PREPARING

for

GLORY

PREPARING *for* GLORY

Biblical Answers to **40 QUESTIONS** *on Living and Dying in Hope of Heaven*

ELIZABETH REYNOLDS TURNAGE

P&R
PUBLISHING
P.O.BOX 817 • PHILLIPSBURG • NEW JERSEY 08865-0817

Scripture quotations from the New Testament use the ESV's alternate, footnoted translation of *adelphoi* ("brothers and sisters").

Italics within Scripture quotations indicate emphasis added.

This book includes stories from the author's life. It reflects the author's present recollections of past experiences. Some names and characteristics have been changed, some events have been compressed, and some dialogue has been re-created.

Cover design by Jelena Mirkovic

Printed in the United States of America

Library of Congress Cataloging-in-Publication Data

Names: Turnage, Elizabeth Reynolds, author.
Title: Preparing for glory : biblical answers to 40 questions on living and dying in hope of heaven / Elizabeth Reynolds Turnage.
Description: Phillipsburg, New Jersey : P&R Publishing, [2024] | Summary: "Life and legacy coach Elizabeth Turnage presents biblical answers to theological and practical questions regarding death, the afterlife, legacy planning, and more-questions relevant to readers at any life stage"-- Provided by publisher.
Identifiers: LCCN 2023040836 | ISBN 9798887790121 (paperback) | ISBN 9798887790138 (epub)
Subjects: LCSH: Future life--Christianity--Miscellanea. | Death--Religious aspects--Christianity. | Heaven--Christianity--Miscellanea.
Classification: LCC BT903 .T87 2024 | DDC 236/.2--dc23/eng/20231023
LC record available at https://lccn.loc.gov/2023040836

In memory of

Mary Jacqueline McIntyre Reynolds

(1938–2021)

Contents

INTRODUCTION

Preparing for Glory

When I tell people I'm studying and writing on the biblical view of death, dying, and eternal life, I sometimes see *the look*. "Why?" says the look. "Are you sick? Are you morbid?" So far, no one has asked these questions out loud, but the look says it all. In case you're wondering too, I assure you—I'm not sick as far as I know, and I'm not morbid (in my opinion).

The reason I wrote this book may be similar to the reason you picked it up. It's the book I've needed as I've ventured repeatedly into the valley of the shadow of death over the last five years or so. In that valley, I've learned how much we need to be able to face our fear of death and dying with the hope of heaven. We need to prepare for death spiritually and practically. We need to know how to grieve with hope. We need to prepare for glory. I'll share a few of my stories from the valley because in them you may find your own.

I saw our need to prepare for glory when my seventy-eight-year-old mom faced a surgery to implant a pacemaker. The night before, she cried as she told me, "I'm afraid to die. I don't know what happens when I die. I don't even know if I'll like being in heaven." My mom was a new believer at the time, and, as is the case for many believers, what she'd heard about heaven didn't convince her she wanted to spend eternity there. My mom needed to know that if she died in surgery, she would immediately wake in the welcoming arms of her Savior. In the hospital with my mom, I saw our need to know the real hope of heaven: the hope of everlasting peace, everlasting joy, and everlasting rest.

I saw our need to prepare for glory when my eighty-one-year-old father was diagnosed with terminal cancer. In the two years before his death, I saw his fear of death and his need for forgiveness. I also saw my own need for wisdom as I encouraged him to prepare an advance directive. I needed him to give me guidance about his end-of-life wishes, because his life was indeed ending. In my father's dying, I saw our need to prepare for death—spiritually, emotionally, and practically.

I saw our need to prepare for glory when our twenty-two-year-old son was diagnosed with a brain tumor and faced four life-threatening surgeries in a seven-month period. In that season, my family needed to know that what we affirmed was true: "My only comfort in life and in death is that I am not my own but belong—body and soul—to my faithful Savior, Jesus Christ."[1] In that harrowing season, I saw that we need to be ready for death at any and every age.

I saw our need to prepare for glory when I received the 2 a.m. phone call that my eighty-three-year-old mother had died unexpectedly of COVID-19. I became the executor of her estate, and, as I navigated numerous details amid deep and complicated grief, I saw our need for practical preparation (she left me the kind gift of a clear guide), and I saw our need for Jesus's companionship on the journey of grief.

There are so many questions we rarely ask and often avoid discussing. What happens when we die? How do we leave legacies that will bless our loved ones when we are incapacitated or die? Do we really believe that our days are numbered? How do we grieve, and how do we help the grieving?

In the valleys of grief, sorrow, and affliction, I have discovered that the Bible offers profound hope. Friend, this life is a millisecond in a marathon. But we are headed toward eternal glory, when every day, day in and day out, we will know the joy for which we were designed: the joy of loving and serving God, the joy of loving and serving one another. When we know the true hope of eternal glory, we will have the courage to face death and dying. We will live intentionally so that we might die intentionally, all to the glory of God.

How to Use This Book

This book is designed to address some common questions and emotions that surround the difficult topics of death and dying. Feel free to turn to the chapters that seem most relevant—they can be taken in any order. Each chapter includes a Scripture verse; a prayer; suggestions for further reading, listening, or watching; a verse from a classic hymn; and a reflection question. Read biblical passages for further encouragement as time allows. If possible, discuss your reading and reflections with others or, at the very least, journal about them.

The "Further Encouragement" resources are linked by QR code for easy access. You can also go to www.prpbooks.com/book/preparing-for-glory to access a list of all the links in the book.

The short Q&A format cannot comprehensively cover every nuance of the complex topics discussed. You will find a bibliography of helpful resources at the back of the book, tagged by topic.

Dear reader, I realize that some of the topics we will consider together may be painful for you, especially if loss is fresh. While I have tried to write with sensitivity about difficult topics, you may find that you need to skip some selections, coming back at another time.

I want you to know that I have prayed for you: that the Holy Spirit would speak to you the words you need to hear, would guide you to the Word you need to know, would comfort you with the comfort of Christ, would strengthen you to face your mortality, and would encourage you with the hope of glory. Jesus is coming soon. What joy we will know in that day.

Part One

Eternal Glory, Death, Christ's Resurrection, and Heaven

1

What is glory, and do we really need to prepare for it?

And after you have suffered a little while, the God of all grace, who has called you to his eternal glory in Christ, will himself restore, confirm, strengthen, and establish you. (1 *Peter* 5:10)

Glory is a wide and weighty word. It is used throughout Scripture to refer to the glory of the triune God. But for the purposes of this book, we are using the word *glory* as many Christian writers did historically, as a shorthand for "eternal glory." I propose this summary of eternal glory:

> Eternal glory is a *place* and an *age* and a *state of glory*
> where glory is given
> to the glorious Father, Son, and Holy Spirit
> by glorified saints
> and where the glory of the Father, Son, and Holy Spirit
> is enjoyed by glorified saints
> for all eternity.

As we see in 1 Peter, we have been called to eternal glory by "the God of all grace . . . in Christ." Eternal glory is the future glory "to be revealed to us" after "the sufferings of this present time" (Rom. 8:18). We and all creation "groan inwardly" as we "wait eagerly" for eternal glory (Rom. 8:23). The sufferings of this world prepare us for eternal glory. Eternal glory is so weighty that it will one day prove our sufferings to have been as light as a feather (see 2 Cor. 4:17–18).

In one sense, of course, we have already inherited this eternal glory if we are in Christ: "Those whom he justified he also glorified" (Rom. 8:30). And yet, our glory's full fruition awaits the day of Christ's return: "When Christ who is your life appears, then you also will appear with him in glory" (Col. 3:4).

Where are we headed? To eternal glory. To heaven, and to the new heavens and the new earth. To looking fully on the face of Christ. To hearing the welcome of our Father and to enjoying the embrace of his Son. To truly believing and clearly seeing God's love for us. To living fully into our creational calling to bear God's image and to rule as servants in Christ's kingdom. And we will do so forever.

As Charles Spurgeon proclaimed, "You and I, when we once enter glory, shall receive what we can neither lose nor leave. Eternity! . . . If you never sang before, yet sing this morning—'God has called us unto his eternal glory,' and this is to be our portion world without end."[1]

Do we need to prepare for eternal glory? If so, why? It is true that in one sense, we are already prepared for eternal glory by our union with Christ. And yet it is an essential part of our journey as Christians to think about, meditate on, wonder about, and practically prepare for the day we will leave this world as we know it to be welcomed by the Father, Son, and Holy Spirit in heaven. When we prepare for glory, we more eagerly anticipate the joys that await us there. When we prepare for glory, we live and leave the legacy that will draw others to the hope of the gospel. When we prepare for glory, we love our friends and family well by giving them clarity to guide them in their season of grief.

> The sands of time are sinking;
> the dawn of heaven breaks;
> the summer morn I've sighed for,
> the fair sweet morn awakes;
> dark, dark has been the midnight,
> but dayspring is at hand,
> and glory, glory dwelleth
> in Emmanuel's land.
> **Anne R. Cousin**

With eternal, everlasting, wondrous joy and glory in mind, we can face the "light and momentary afflictions" of death and dying, aging and illness, grief and loss. We can learn about death's beginning and death's end. We can explore our future state in heaven and our forever state in the new heavens and the new earth. And yes, we can face the agonizing reality of judgment and hell.

We can get practical about our possessions, and we can make end-of-life plans to lessen our loved ones' burden of grief and guilt. We can forgive and ask forgiveness, we can say thank-you, and we can share our stories of redemption. We can learn how to lament, and we can step into the journey of grief. While these tasks may intimidate us, we can approach them confidently with the hope of eternal glory. I invite you to join me in this wonderful journey.

PRAYER

Eternal and triune God, how we look forward to the day we will join you in eternal glory. Enliven our imaginations so that we can anticipate that day with joy. Encourage our hearts so that we can prepare for such glory, both spiritually and practically. In Jesus's glorious name, amen.

FURTHER ENCOURAGEMENT

Read Romans 8:18–25; 2 Corinthians 4:16–18; 1 Peter 5:10–11.
Read "Glory" by Charles Spurgeon.

FOR REFLECTION

How may thoughts of your future in eternal glory encourage your heart as you consider facing death?

2

Why do people have to die?

And the LORD *God commanded the man, saying, "You may surely eat of every tree of the garden, but of the tree of the knowledge of good and evil you shall not eat, for in the day that you eat of it you shall surely die."* (*Gen.* 2:16–2:17)

Why did she have to die? Even though my mother was eighty-three years old when she died, and even though she had lived a full and long life, I still asked this question. In our heartache, many of us have raised the seemingly unanswerable question—if God loves us, why do we die? We cannot soothe the fiery pain behind this question, but as we see God's merciful response to the sin that introduced death into the world, we find hope for redemption even in the curse of death.

In the beginning, God formed Adam from the dust, Eve from Adam's rib, breathing life into the first man and woman and shaping them in his image, with the potential to live forever (see Gen. 1:26–27; 2:7). He called them "very good" (1:31). God generously invited Adam and Eve to eat from every tree of the garden except for the tree of the knowledge of good and evil (see 2:16–17). If they disobeyed his command and ate from that tree, he warned, they would die (see v. 17).

Genesis 3:1–6 tells us how the serpent, Satan embodied, approached Eve (and Adam, who likely was standing right beside her), tempting her to eat from the only forbidden tree. When she objected, the serpent scoffed: "You will not surely die" (v. 4). Adam and Eve did eat the fruit of the tree, but they did not die physically—at least not immediately. Instead, their eyes were opened, they discovered they were naked, and they felt shame. They hid from God as he walked through the garden seeking them.

As it turned out, the first death was a spiritual one that broke the relationship between God and his beloved creation. And yet, through sin, physical death would also enter the world (see Rom. 5:12).

If the story had ended here, there would be little point for us to prepare for death and dying. But by God's grace, it did not. Even before God told Adam and Eve the consequences of their sin, he addressed Satan, telling him that he would one day send a child to crush him (see Gen. 3:15). Genesis 3:15 is the first proclamation of the gospel hope in Scripture. We know this promised child would be God's own Son, Jesus Christ, and he would defeat Satan forever by dying on a cross. Death itself would be redeemed by his sacrifice.

O Christ, be thou our lasting joy,
our ever great reward!
Our only glory may it be
to glory in the Lord.
John Chandler

We should grieve death and dying. Death is unnatural—it is one of the devastating consequences of the fall. And yet, because God allowed his own Son to die, God's people have hope. It is in this hope that we can face the harsh reality of death and dying.

PRAYER

Creator God, thank you for making us in your image, for shaping us for life forever with you. Thank you for providing a way out of sin and death through the death and resurrection of your beloved Son, Jesus. As we prepare for dying and death, may we hold tightly to the hope we have in him. In the name of the resurrected Christ we pray, amen.

FURTHER ENCOURAGEMENT

Read Genesis 1–3.
Read "Why Must We Die?" by Eddie Mercado.

FOR REFLECTION

God planned for the redemption of death even as humanity's sin brought death into the world. How might this encourage you?

3

How was death defeated?

Our Savior Christ Jesus . . . abolished death and brought life and immortality to light through the gospel. (2 *Tim.* 1:10)

Imagine an evil king who locks victims in the dungeon of his castle, holding them captive to the fear that he may kill them at any time. Scripture tells us Satan is like that evil king. Although God ultimately rules over Satan, Satan has held God's people in "lifelong slavery" through the "fear of death" (Heb. 2:15).

To rescue us from death, we needed a hero—but not just any hero would do. The hero had to be a perfectly holy man, completely without sin. There is only one such hero, and that is the One who came to abolish death.

> To him I owe my life and breath,
> and all the joys I have;
> He makes me triumph over death,
> and saves me from the grave.
> **Samuel Stennett**

The hero, our Savior Jesus Christ, came into the world as a baby: "though he was in the form of God," he submitted to being "born in the likeness of men" (Phil. 2:6, 7). He walked this earth in human flesh, knowing his life would end in mockery and shame on a cursed cross. Though he was tempted by Satan in the wilderness, he never sinned, and as a sinless human, he became the perfect sacrifice for our sins.

In Gethsemane, on the night before his death, Jesus cried out in anguish and even sweat blood, grieving the horror of the death he came to die (see Luke 22:44). And yet he surrendered to the Father's plan, saying, "Not my will, but yours, be done" (v. 42). On the cross, Christ "tasted death" for us (Heb. 2:9), redeeming us from our captivity to sin and death: "He entered once for all into the holy places, not by means of the blood of goats and calves, but by means of his own blood, thus securing an eternal redemption" (9:12). When he died on the cross for our sins, Christ "disarmed the rulers and authorities and put them to open shame, by triumphing over them" (Col. 2:15). Through his own death, Jesus "destroy[ed] the one who has the power of death, that is, the devil" (Heb. 2:14).

"Yes," you may say, "but we still die." Perhaps death has taken your friend, your spouse, your child, your coworker. Has death really been defeated? We need to know more of the story: Christ defeated death not only by dying but also by being raised from the dead. But for today, dear friend, let's camp out in the good news that, as we face death and dying, we are united to the One who has gone before us. In him, we will never have to face death and dying alone.

PRAYER

Precious Jesus, thank you for surrendering yourself in humility to the only plan of redemption that would truly free us from our captivity to sin and death. Thank you for enduring the cross for us, though you despised its shame, because you looked forward to the joy of reconciling us to the Father. In your sinless name, amen.

FURTHER ENCOURAGEMENT

Read Colossians 2:15; Hebrews 2:9–18; 9:11–28.
Read "The Death of Death in the Death of Christ Means Victory over Death for Those Who Believe" by Thabiti Anyabwile.

FOR REFLECTION

Consider Christ's death on the cross. How does it make you feel to know that he has "tasted death" for you—that he has gone before you in suffering and dying?

4

What hope does the resurrection of Christ give us?

If Christ has not been raised, your faith is futile, and you are still in your sins. (1 *Cor.* 15:17)

A 2017 study revealed that 25 percent of British people who identified as Christians at that time did not believe in the resurrection of Jesus.[1] And yet, as pastor and theologian Stephen Um explains, even atheist scholars find weighty evidence for the resurrection. Um quotes atheist philosopher Antony Flew: "The evidence for the resurrection is better than for claimed miracles in any other religion."[2] The resurrection is central to the gospel: if the resurrection didn't happen, Paul tells the doubting Corinthians, our hope in Christ is pitiable (see 1 Cor. 15:19).

On the first Good Friday, Jesus spent his last breath. To confirm his death, a Roman soldier pierced his side with a spear. With the permission of Pilate, a man named Joseph of Arimathea took Jesus's body from the cross, wrapped it in a linen shroud, and buried it in his tomb (see Mark 15:42–46).

Christ's followers were deeply grieved and confused the next day—the One they had thought would save them had died. How could it be? The disciples had never fully understood what he meant when he said, "The Son of Man is about to be delivered into the hands of men, and they will kill him, and he will be raised on the third day" (Matt. 17:22–23).

And then he appeared in a new body—a resurrected body. Many saw him:

- the women who went to the tomb to finish preparing the body for burial (see Mark 16:1)
- Mary Magdalene, who mistook Jesus for the gardener (see John 20:15)
- Thomas, who, at Jesus's command, touched Jesus's nail-scarred hands (see John 20:24–27)
- the disciples, who trembled together in a locked room when Jesus suddenly stood among them, saying, "Peace be with you" (John 20:19)

And that's not all. Many more saw Jesus as he walked the earth in his resurrected body for forty days before ascending to heaven.

The apostle Paul insists that the resurrection of Christ is at the heart of the gospel. If it didn't actually happen, he says, "then those also who have fallen asleep in Christ have perished" (1 Cor. 15:18). If it did, then the effects of the curse of Adam's sin have been reversed: "For as in Adam all die, so also in Christ shall all be made alive" (v. 22).

Because of Christ's resurrection, we have hope for our loved ones who die in Christ. Those who trust in Christ are united to him by faith. Although we were once dead in our sins, we are now spiritually alive in Christ. When we die, we will be with Christ (see 2 Cor. 5:6–8). When Christ returns in glory, those who have already died, as well as those who are still alive, will be given new, immortal bodies in which we will live forever. This is the sure hope provided by Christ's resurrection.

> Soar we now where Christ has led,
> following our exalted Head.
> Made like him, like him we rise!
> Ours the cross, the grave, the skies!
> **Charles Wesley**

PRAYER

Resurrected Jesus, in our skeptical age, we are bombarded with temptations to disbelieve your miraculous resurrection. By your Spirit, give us the faith to believe that which we cannot see. We have been made alive in you, and one day we will live forever because of your resurrection. In your trustworthy name, amen.

FURTHER ENCOURAGEMENT

Read Matthew 28:1–15; 1 Corinthians 15:1–19.
Watch the sermon "Resurrection" by Stephen Um.

FOR REFLECTION

Christ truly was raised from the dead. How does this change everything you would otherwise believe about death and eternal life?

5

What happens to us when we die?

And if I go and prepare a place for you, I will come again and will take you to myself, that where I am you may be also.
(*John* 14:3)

As Keisha's father neared death from lung cancer, hospice nurses alerted her to signs of approaching death she might notice in his final days and hours. They told her to look for changes in breathing, activity level, appetite, and thirst. Sadly, the nurses offered no answers to Keisha's deeper question—what would happen to her father spiritually when he died? She knew he was a Christian. She wondered if he would go immediately to heaven and what heaven would be like.

The Bible offers Keisha the comfort that her father was ushered into the presence of the Lord the moment he died. Jesus tells the converted thief on the cross, "*Today* you will be with me in paradise" (Luke 23:43). According to Jesus, angels escort people to heaven: "The poor man died and was carried by the angels to Abraham's side" (Luke 16:22). As

Philip Ryken points out, God knows our fear of death and in compassion sends his angels to comfort us in this most dreaded moment.[1]

We are comforted to know that our souls will be with the Lord when we die. And yet, this will not be our final state, because one day Christ will come to establish the new heavens and the new earth, and in that day, our bodies will also be raised. Since the state we enter immediately after our death is temporary, theologians call it the *intermediate* or *interim* state.

While we may wonder about the location and the nature of this intermediate state, Scripture provides only a few clues. As we saw, Jesus calls it "paradise" (Luke 23:43). The word *paradise* is used in the New Testament to refer to "a place of blessedness where God dwells."[2] In the Old Testament, *paradise* refers to the garden of Eden. Thus, heaven is a place of perfect beauty, flourishing, and wholeness where the presence of God is fully known.

Jesus also gives a few clues about what heaven is like, telling the disciples he is going to prepare "a place" for them in his "Father's house" (John 14:2). Think of it! Just as I prepare my home for guests by making the beds and dusting the furniture and putting out little treats, Christ, our host, prepares our welcome in heaven. While we may not know precisely what heaven will be like, we can be sure that it will feel more like home than any home we have ever known.

Dearest Lord, thee will I cherish.
Though my breath fail in death,
yet I shall not perish,
but with thee abide for ever
there on high, in that joy
which can vanish never.
Paul Gerhardt

According to Scripture, the greatest joy of the intermediate state is being in the presence of the Lord: "We would rather be away from the body and at home with the Lord" (2 Cor. 5:8). As the apostle Paul anticipated his own death, he proclaimed, "My desire is to depart and be with Christ, for that is far better" (Phil. 1:23).

Our desire for heaven grows as we imagine meeting the triune God there. What welcome we will receive! Just imagine burying your face in Jesus's shoulder and telling him how hard chemo was. Just imagine hearing your Father say, "Come, child! I'm glad you're home!" Oh, what a day that will be!

PRAYER

Heavenly Father, stir our longings to be with you in heaven. Help us to imagine the perfect peace and the indescribable joy we will know when we depart this fallen world and go home to be with you. In Jesus's holy name, amen.

FURTHER ENCOURAGEMENT

Read Philippians 1:23; 2 Corinthians 5:8; Revelation 4:1–11.
Read "Death and the Intermediate State" from Ligonier.

FOR REFLECTION

What excites you most about being in the presence of the Lord?

6

Do we become angels when we die?

Are they not all ministering spirits sent out to serve for the sake of those who are to inherit salvation? (*Heb.* 1:14)

We've all seen the image on social media or on a greeting card. The background contains either a white angel with feathery wings or large, fluffy clouds or both. A flowing cursive script reads, "Heaven has gained another angel." No wonder we are a little confused about what we become when we die.

To address the common misconception that humans become angels after death, we need to know what the Bible says about angels and how they differ from humans. Once we understand the difference, we will more eagerly anticipate joining the angels in heaven to worship God.

Angels are spirit beings created by God to serve human beings (see Ps. 148:2, 5; Heb. 1:14). Some angels chose to rebel against God: "Having joined Satan's rebellion, they were cast out of heaven to await final judgment."[1] The angels who did not rebel remain in heaven as immortal and glorious beings who worship God and serve mankind (see Ps. 103:20–21; Luke 1:19; Heb. 1:14). There are many angels—Revelation 5:11 speaks of "myriads of myriads," and Hebrews 12:22 says they are "innumerable." Even though their numbers are great, they will neither increase nor decrease, for angels do not marry, reproduce, or die (see Luke 20:36).

Angels have individual identities and personal names. Sometimes they take on physical form to deliver messages on earth: the angel Gabriel, as we know, visited both Zechariah and Mary to tell them about the births of two unexpected babies (see Luke 1:8–23, 26–38). When angels visit in physical form, humans are almost always frightened; it is unlikely that angels are blond-haired, chubby-cheeked babies!

As they serve humans, angels often act as guardians and protectors: Jesus said, "See that you do not despise one of these little ones. For I tell you that in heaven their angels always see the face of my Father who is in heaven" (Matt. 18:10). Angels cared for Jesus after he was tempted in the wilderness (see Matt. 4:11), and an angel ministered to him when he wept and prayed in Gethsemane before going to the cross (see Luke 22:43).

> Angels, sing on, your faithful watches keeping,
> sing us sweet fragments of the songs above,
> till morning's joy shall end the night of weeping
> and life's long shadows break in cloudless love.
> **Frederick William Faber**

If angels are so different from humans, why do some people think we become angels when we die? The confusion may stem from the fact that humans do not have bodies in the intermediate state after death. Yet we will receive redeemed and restored bodies when Jesus returns—angels will not. They will never become physical beings because God created them to be spirits.

In addition, in the new heavens and the new earth, humans will no longer be "lower than the angels" (Ps. 8:5 NIV), for we will take part in the final judgment, judging even the angels (see 1 Cor. 6:3). We will be glorious like the angels, yet we will be redeemed, adopted children of the Father. We will be like Jesus (see 1 John 3:2). Finally, in the new heavens and the new earth, humans will fulfill their creational purpose of having dominion over the earth: "The one who conquers, I will grant him to sit with me on the throne" (Rev. 3:21). Angels were not created for dominion and will never be given this authority.

Dear friend, a far better future awaits us than "receiving our angel wings." Let us anticipate the glorious day when we will receive our resurrection bodies and become everything our Creator designed us to be.

PRAYER

Heavenly Father, thank you for making us different from the angels and for giving us angels to guard and guide us. How we look forward to the day when we will join with the angels in worshiping you in heaven. Amen.

FURTHER ENCOURAGEMENT

Read Psalm 148:2–5; Matthew 18:10; Luke 22:43; Hebrews 1:14. **Read** "People Aren't Downgraded to Angels When They Die" by Chad Bird.

FOR REFLECTION

Have you ever wondered whether humans become angels when they die? What hope does it bring to know you will not become an angel in heaven?

7

What is life like in heaven?

Around the throne were twenty-four thrones, and seated on the thrones were twenty-four elders, clothed in white garments, with golden crowns on their heads. (*Rev.* 4:4)

Too many of us dread an eternity of floating on clouds, playing harps, and singing stale worship music. When we understand what life will really be like in heaven, we will no longer fear that we face everlasting boredom. Let's consider four aspects of life in heaven.

Reunion. In heaven, we will have the surpassing joy of reuniting with the Lord (see Phil. 1:23). Because God is a relational God, we also have reason to hope that we will be reunited with the loved ones who have gone before us to heaven. Although there will be no marriage there (see Luke 20:35), the Bible does suggest

> Be still, my soul;
> the hour is hast'ning on
> when we shall be
> forever with the Lord,
> when disappointment, grief,
> and fear are gone,
> sorrow forgot,
> love's purest joys restored.
> **Kathrina von Schlegel**

that in heaven we will recognize and relate to those we knew on earth, as well as those we didn't. For example, the disciples were able to recognize Moses and Elijah at the transfiguration, and the rich man recognized Lazarus (see Matt. 17:1–3; Luke 16:19–31).

Worship. Worship is another surpassing joy of heaven. If we fear that eternal worship will be boring, it is probably because we've had a poor earthly experience of worship and thus can't grasp the beauty of heavenly worship. The saints who surround the throne in heaven fall down before God, praising him: "You created all things, and by your will they existed and were created" (Rev. 4:11). In heaven, there will be no more worship wars—no more quibbling over praise songs or hymns. We will be in the full presence of the God who created the cosmos, the God who sent his sinless Son to die that we might live with him forever. The question in heaven will truly be "How can we *keep* from singing?"

> Be still, my soul;
> when change and tears are past,
> all safe and blessed
> we shall meet at last.
> **Kathrina von Schlegel**

Prayer. Further, in the intermediate state, we will pray as never before. Prayer is simply communicating with God, and in heaven, we will be in the unbroken presence of the Lord. Revelation 5:8 refers to the "prayers of the saints," and in Revelation 6, those who have suffered on earth pray for justice: "O Sovereign Lord, holy and true, how long before you will judge and avenge our blood on those who dwell on the earth?" (v. 10). In the intermediate state, we will join with Jesus in praying for the healing and restoration of the fallen world.

Rest. We will not only pray but also rest. In response to their prayer, the martyrs "were each given a white robe and told to rest a little longer" (Rev. 6:11). Though we were granted rest from our slavery to sin and death when we trusted in Christ (see Rom. 6:14), we will know this rest perfectly in heaven (see Rev. 14:13). In this fallen world, we often struggle to embrace God's gift of rest, but in heaven we will enjoy it fully.

Dear friend, we need not fear boredom or loneliness in heaven. We will be in the presence of God and other believers, dwelling in glory, and we won't be able to contain our joy, our awe, our love, and our excitement!

PRAYER

Father, Son, and Holy Spirit, enliven our imaginations, fuel our anticipation of heaven. Increase our desire to dwell with you in glory, so that we, like Paul, will be able to say, "To live is Christ . . . to die is gain" (Phil. 1:21). In Jesus's name, amen.

FURTHER ENCOURAGEMENT

Read Luke 9:28–36; 16:19–31; Revelation 4:1–11; 6:9–11.
Read "Heaven Will Never Be Boring" by Dave Radford.

FOR REFLECTION

Write a prayer of gratitude and worship, thanking God for the joys you anticipate in heaven.

PART TWO

The Day of the Lord, the New Heavens and the New Earth, and the Final Judgment

8

What is the "day of the Lord"?

Then we who are alive, who are left, will be caught up together with them in the clouds to meet the Lord in the air, and so we will always be with the Lord. (1 *Thess.* 4:17)

I turn sixty in a few months. Suppose my family told me today that they plan to throw me a surprise birthday party sometime soon. On that day, all four of my children, my three children-in-law, and my grandchildren will parade into my house with a marching band, collect my husband and me, climb into a luxurious minibus, gather a few more friends, and head to an undisclosed (to me) paradise to celebrate. Wouldn't I be excited? Wouldn't I wait for that day, wondering when it would be, daydreaming about it, and imagining the joy it would bring?

For Christians, the day of the Lord—the day the Lord Jesus returns—should spark a similar anticipation. The apostle Paul's first letter to the Thessalonians teaches us how to wait for that day. The Thessalonian believers were discouraged and confused following the deaths of some fellow Christians. Paul reassured them that they need not grieve as those who have no hope (see 4:13), and he told them about the coming day of the Lord.

> O Lord, haste the day
> when my faith shall be sight,
> the clouds be rolled back as a scroll;
> the trump shall resound
> and the Lord shall descend;
> even so, it is well with my soul.
> **Horatio Gates Spafford**

Jesus will come from heaven, "with a cry of command, with the voice of an archangel, and with the sound of the trumpet of God" (v. 16). Jesus's return will be noisy and sudden, and we don't know when to expect it. When Jesus returns, he will first raise the bodies of those who have already died in Christ (see v. 16). Then he will raise the living, and we will go together to meet Christ and escort him back to earth, where he will establish his kingdom: the new heavens and the new earth (see v. 17). On this day, the intermediate state ends, and eternal glory begins. All believers, both those who have already died and those who are still alive, will be given resurrection bodies that are perfectly suited to their new lives in the new heavens and the new earth.

Paul encouraged the Thessalonian Christians to look forward to the day of the Lord. For "children of light" (5:5), the day of Christ's return will be a glorious day of reunion and celebration. It is true that for unbelievers, Christ's return will come like a "thief in the night" (5:2) and will be a "day of wrath when God's righteous judgment will be revealed" (Rom. 2:5). But for those who are found in Christ, it will be a "day of redemption" (Eph. 4:30).

How do we prepare for the day of the Lord? In anticipation of that day, which Jesus says is "coming soon" (Rev. 22:7), we grow in faith, in hope, and in love, as we share the good news of our resurrection hope (see 1 Thess. 5:8).

PRAYER

Precious Lord Jesus, how we long for the day of your return! Although Scripture tells us that no one knows when this day will come, help us to eagerly anticipate it, to be encouraged by this day of hope in times of sorrow or trouble. In your name, amen.

FURTHER ENCOURAGEMENT

Read 1 Thessalonians 4:13–5:11.
Watch "Book of 1 Thessalonians Summary" by BibleProject.

FOR REFLECTION

What questions, fears, or hopes do you have about the day of the Lord?

9

What does Christ's resurrection mean for the future of our bodies?

For as in Adam all die, so also in Christ shall all be made alive. But each in his own order: Christ the firstfruits, then at his coming those who belong to Christ. (1 *Cor.* 15:22–23)

Perhaps you've heard of cryonic preservation: "Freezing a body and then reanimating it in the future."[1] As science writer Kate Golembiewski asks, "If it worked for Han Solo, Captain America, and Fry from *Futurama*, why can't it work for us?"[2] However, the technology we need to restore a dead body by freezing and later thawing it simply does not exist today.[3] Christians have a far better and more believable hope—the resurrection of the body.

And yet, we, like the Corinthians, struggle to grasp how a dead, decomposed body could ever become a living, breathing, resurrected body. The apostle Paul uses the analogy of a seed to explain this mysterious transformation. Just as a seed buried in the ground eventually emerges as a stalk of wheat, so will our dead bodies be transformed by God when he raises us to new life (see 1 Cor. 15:36–37). Our resurrection bodies will be essentially the same bodies as our perishable bodies, but in eternity, they will be "imperishable" (1 Cor. 15:42).

To understand what our resurrection bodies will be like, we have only to remember Christ, the "firstfruits" (1 Cor. 15:23). His resurrected body was physical: his voice was recognizable, his hands bore the scars of the cross, his appetite for fish remained. As theologian Paul Williamson explains, "If Christ's resurrection body is the archetype, then the resurrection body appears to be a suitably remodeled and enhanced version of the one we now occupy."[4]

Unlike Christ, we do not receive our resurrection bodies immediately after our death. Our physical bodies will die and decay; our spirits will go immediately to be with Jesus in heaven. There, we will enjoy the presence of God and other saints who died before us. But we await the final day of full resurrection.

When this poor lisping,
stamm'ring tongue
lies silent in the grave,
then in a nobler, sweeter song
I'll sing thy pow'r to save.
William Cowper

On that day, "the trumpet will sound, and the dead will be raised imperishable, and we shall be changed" (1 Cor. 15:52). On that day, Jesus will return, the "dead in Christ will rise first" (1 Thess. 4:16–17), and "this mortal body [will] put on immortality" (1 Cor. 15:53). Believers who are still alive when Jesus returns will join in this great cloud of glory, and we will all dwell together with God in the new heavens and the new earth (see 1 Thess. 4:16–17; Rev. 21:1–5). In that day, we will serve God forever in our resurrection bodies—with our hands, our feet, and our voices.

Dear friend, even as we consider our certain mortality, we have a great hope that awaits: the hope of living with

God and fellow saints forever in our resurrected bodies. Let's live with resurrection joy as we consider the day when we will truly dance as the bride of Christ.

PRAYER

Lord, we've never seen a resurrected body, so we are puzzled about what ours will be like. Remind us of our resurrected Lord and help us to see in him the glorious future that awaits all who belong to you. In the name of the resurrected Christ, amen.

FURTHER ENCOURAGEMENT

Read 1 Corinthians 15:35–58.
Watch "Resurrection: The Ultimate Makeover?" by Paul Williamson.

FOR REFLECTION

What misconceptions have you heard or had about your resurrected body? What about living in your resurrection body excites you?

10

What are the new heavens and the new earth?

Then I saw a new heaven and a new earth, for the first heaven and the first earth had passed away, and the sea was no more. (*Rev.* 21:1)

The intermediate state gives way to our final state, described by theologian N. T. Wright as "life after life-after-death."[1] What is life in eternity like? Think of the best adventure movie you've ever seen. The battle is won, the bad guys defeated. After the final image fades, a new screen appears: "Five years later . . ." Now you see victorious soldiers sit down with their beloved captain, enjoy a feast with the entire village, hug their children and grandchildren, and tend a garden with their neighbors.

If you can picture this, you are getting a glimpse of the scene in Revelation 21 and 22. The battle has ended, Jesus has won, and Satan and all his worshipers have been tossed into the lake of fire (see Rev. 20:7–10). Now our real life, our truest life, the life we have been waiting for all along, begins.

John saw this new life because he was looking for it. What will we see when we begin looking for it?

We will see what John saw: a new heaven and a new earth. Throughout Scripture, the phrase *heaven and earth* refers to the entire cosmos, the material and spiritual world. In Revelation 21:1, the heaven and the earth are "new" (*kainos* in Greek), that is, "new in nature" (which implies "better").[2] The new heaven and the new earth are the old heaven and the old earth fully transformed.

But what about the first heaven and the first earth? They have "passed away" (Rev. 21:1). Author Nathan Bierma explains, "As with metal in a white-hot furnace, all impurities, deformities, and corruptions of planet earth will meet their fiery demise. All that will remain is goodness."[3] The fire of 2 Peter 3:10—if, indeed, it is a literal fire—will purify and refine, leaving behind only what is glorious and glorifying. In this way, "the creation itself will be set free from its bondage to corruption and obtain the freedom of the glory of the children of God" (Rom. 8:21).

> The goodly land I see
> with peace and plenty blest,
> a land of sacred liberty
> and endless rest.
> There milk and honey flow,
> and oil and wine abound,
> and trees of life forever grow,
> with mercy crowned.
> **Thomas Olivers**

Someday, we will live forever in a very physical world, a world that has been fully redeemed and restored, one characterized by *shalom*—that is, a state of harmony, unity, wholeness, and flourishing. The new heavens and the new earth are coming soon to a neighborhood near us—in fact, to our very own neighborhoods. In anticipation of the shalom to come, we seek to restore shalom in our homes, our workplaces, and our communities today.

PRAYER

Holy God, Creator of the cosmos, show us the end of our story, the end that begins our truest story, our story of living and loving in a whole, healed, and harmonious new heaven and new earth. In the name of our Redeemer we ask these things, amen.

FURTHER ENCOURAGEMENT

Read Romans 8:21; 2 Peter 3:8–13; Revelation 21:1.
Read "Heaven Is a Place on Earth: 3 Reasons from 2 Peter 3" from P&R Publishing.

FOR REFLECTION

Have you ever heard people say, "It's all going to burn," meaning that the earth will be burned and cease to exist? Considering the Scripture cited in this chapter, what gives you hope that the current creation will not be destroyed but transformed?

11

What will life be like in the new heavens and the new earth?

I saw the holy city, new Jerusalem, coming down out of heaven from God, prepared as a bride adorned for her husband.
(*Rev.* 21:2)

On June 2, 2003, the fiftieth anniversary of Queen Elizabeth's coronation, nine-year-old Louisa Harrington, a cardiomyopathy patient, was granted her wish—to meet the queen. Invited by the queen to present her with a bouquet of flowers after the coronation anniversary service, little Louisa was ecstatic.[1] Can you imagine her trying to describe the sights and sounds of that day to her friends? She must have been so excited that her words came out in a jumble.

This must be how the apostle John felt as he tried to describe what he saw when the angel showed him the new heavens and the new earth. It's a garden! It's a city! It's a temple! No, wait—it's a bride! John was overwhelmed by glory, and I pray that we will also be overwhelmed by our glorious future as we explore life in the new heavens and the new earth.

The new heavens and the new earth are a city—a different kind of city, a city whose lights shine eternally with a glory that never loses its luster. It's a holy city, not an ancient city, or a global city, or a magic city, but a *holy* city, a city set apart for God's glory. It is the "new" Jerusalem, coming down out of heaven from God, not built up from the ground by man.

In that city, there will be no more sorrow, no more pain, no more death, no more evil, no more corruption, no more sin, and no more darkness (see Rev. 21:4, 8, 25, 27). If sin brought death and decay into the world, spoiling the shalom—the harmony and flourishing—God created, then the new heavens and the new earth will reverse these effects and restore shalom.

O the deep, deep love of Jesus!
Love of ev'ry love the best:
'tis an ocean vast of blessing,
'tis a haven sweet of rest.
O the deep, deep love of Jesus!
'Tis a heav'n of heav'ns to me;
and it lifts me up to glory,
for it lifts me up to thee.
Samuel Travor Francis

Some good things will no longer exist in the city because their present versions are only a mirror of the glory that awaits us. There will be no more marriage because we, the church, are the bride, and we are intimately known by the triune God (see v. 2). There will be no more temple because the city is shaped like the Holy of Holies; in other words, it *is* the temple—where we live is where we worship (see 21:22; 22:4).

There will, however, be perfect relationships, perfect diversity, perfect unity, perfect work, perfect nature, perfect feasting, perfect health, and perfect worship. The tree of life will grow tall and broad beside the river of life, which flows through the city (see 22:1–2). Kings and queens from every city, country, and continent will parade through the glorious city (see 21:24); they will gather at lavish victory feasts to tell the story of how Christ the King rescued them (see Rev. 19). In fact, we will all be royals there, reigning with King Jesus in the eternal service of worship.

Dear friend, let us long for the day when we will finally look on the face of Christ, seeing him as he really is, and becoming like him in everlasting glory (see 22:4; 1 John 3:2).

PRAYER

Glorious Christ, how we anticipate the day when we will see your glorious face and will be made like you. Give us the eyes to see how everything around us will be gloriously restored in that day. In your renewing name, amen.

FURTHER ENCOURAGEMENT

Read Revelation 21–22.
Read "Former Things" by Scotty Smith.

FOR REFLECTION

Read slowly through Revelation 21 and 22. Take note of all the things that excite you about life in the new heavens and the new earth.

12

What happens to the believer on the day of judgment?

I saw the dead, great and small, standing before the throne, and books were opened. Then another book was opened, which is the book of life. And the dead were judged by what was written in the books, according to what they had done. (*Rev.* 20:12)

There is perhaps no more ridiculed, poorly explained, or grossly misrepresented doctrine than that of "judgment day." For years, I lived in dread of standing before God while my every cruel thought, hidden sin, and past rebellion played like a horror movie on a large screen. As we look at what Scripture says about the final judgment, we discover good news: believers will be judged according to the Holy Spirit's work in us, and we will be judged by Jesus, the one who cried from the cross, "It is finished" (John 19:30). As theologian Richard Phillips says, "No Christian, justified through faith in Christ, should ever face the thought of the final judgment with . . . anxiety."[1]

Because we are "justified by faith apart from works of the law" (Rom. 3:28), and because those who are joined to Christ by faith become the "righteousness of God" (2 Cor. 5:21), we know that judgment day will not be a day of condemnation for believers (see Rom. 8:1). The book of life that is opened in Revelation 20:12 is the "book of life of the Lamb who was slain" (Rev. 13:8), and Jesus will "confess" the names written therein "before [his] Father and before his angels" (Rev. 3:5). Those whose names are written in the book of life have eternal security and a glorious future in the new heavens and the new earth.

What, then, will be revealed in the *books* that are opened as believers stand before the throne? These books reveal our deeds—both our sins and our service to Christ. And yet, we need not fear, for where sin after sin is listed, the pages are "stamped with words like 'forgiven,' 'pardoned,' 'cancelled.'"[2] The books of our deeds also confirm our connection to Christ, as Nancy Guthrie explains: "The books will show how you threw yourself on his mercy and welcomed his forgiveness, how your appetites and affections changed."[3]

Bold shall I stand in thy great day,
for who aught to my charge shall lay?
While thro' thy blood absolv'd I am,
from sin's tremendous curse and shame.
Nikolaus Ludwig von Zinzendorf

Rather than being condemned on the day of final judgment, we will receive our reward, our inheritance, the kingdom of God (see Matt. 25:34). Dear saint, hidden in Christ, you need not fear the day of judgment. There is truly "no condemnation for those who are in Christ Jesus" (Rom. 8:1). Not now. Not ever.

PRAYER

Holy and just God, show us the depth of your love for us in Jesus. Because Jesus bore the punishment for our sins on the cross, we have the hope of glory. May we eagerly anticipate the day when we will hear your voice of welcome, the day when we will receive the crowns we most surely don't deserve. In Jesus's saving name, amen.

FURTHER ENCOURAGEMENT

Read Matthew 25:31–40; Romans 3:28; 2 Corinthians 5:21; Revelation 3:5; 13:8; 20:11–15.
Listen to "Q&R on the Book of Revelation" with Darrell Johnson and Tim Hughes.

FOR REFLECTION

What fears or concerns do you have about the final judgment? All who trust in Christ need face no condemnation on that day—what does this truth do for your concerns?

13

What happens to the unbeliever on the day of judgment?

But because of your hard and impenitent heart you are storing up wrath for yourself on the day of wrath when God's righteous judgment will be revealed. (Rom. 2:5)

The final judgment of unbelievers troubled me deeply when I became a Christian, especially because my own parents weren't followers of Christ.[1] Many believers are concerned for their unbelieving loved ones, and it is painful to imagine God's judgment of unbelieving family and friends. How do we cope when God's just judgment and his righteous wrath against evil and unbelieving people are clearly taught throughout Scripture? As we study God's wrath and the final judgment, we will learn how to live more faithfully in light of eternity.

What is God's wrath? It is "a right and necessary reaction to objective moral evil."[2] God's wrath is rooted in his perfectly holy, perfectly just, perfectly loving, perfectly merciful character. God's wrath bears no resemblance to the violent, unpredictable, and abusive anger of some humans. God's wrath is his "*righteous* judgment" (Rom. 2:5)—the just judgment of a holy God.

In his wrath, God is "patient" (2 Peter 3:8–9), "slow to anger" (Nah. 1:3), and "abounding in steadfast love" (Ps. 103:8). God the Son—in the greatest mystery of all—drank the cup of his Father's wrath on the cross, bearing the full punishment for the sins of all who would trust in him for salvation. God's wrath is never separate from his love; as Jonathan Edwards observed, "God has no pleasure in the destruction or calamity of persons or people. . . . He is a God that delights in mercy, and judgment is his strange work."[3]

With this understanding of God's wrath in mind, consider the day of judgment once more. On that day, unbelievers will also stand before the great white throne (see Rev. 20:11). Books will be opened—but there will be no stamp to mark unbelievers as forgiven or pardoned. Seeing the light, they "loved the darkness . . . because their works were evil" (John 3:19). As theologian J. I. Packer explains, "The unbeliever has preferred to be by himself, without God, defying God, having God against him, and he shall have his preference."[4]

How then do we respond to God's wrath against unbelievers in the final judgment? We begin by recognizing and confessing our own sin, knowing that without Christ, we too would deserve God's wrath. Doing so leads us to be more grateful for the gift of salvation and more awed by God's holiness. God's wrath can bring comfort when we or those we love are victims of evil; rather than taking

At his call the dead awaken,
rise to life from earth and sea;
all the pow'rs of nature, shaken
by his looks, prepare to flee.
Careless sinner,
what will then become of thee?
John Newton

vengeance ourselves, we can trust God to judge evil. Finally, knowing the day of judgment is coming, we eagerly share the gospel with unbelievers, remembering that God is merciful and slow to anger.[5]

Dear friend, how shall we prepare for eternal glory? By having our hearts broken over our own sin and by having our hearts stirred to share the hope of eternity with those who do not know God.

PRAYER

Holy and merciful God, stir our hearts that we might long for your justice against evil, and forgive us for our apathy. May we eagerly share the hope of Christ with all who do not trust in him for salvation. In Jesus's saving name, amen.

FURTHER ENCOURAGEMENT

Read Romans 2:1–11; 2 Peter 3:8–9; Revelation 20:11–15.
Watch "The Comfort of God's Judgment and Justice" by Nancy Guthrie.

FOR REFLECTION

What have you learned about God's wrath and his judgment of unbelievers? If you struggle with these teachings, write your struggles in an honest prayer.

14

Is hell real, and if so, what is it like?

And the smoke of their torment goes up forever and ever, and they have no rest, day or night. (*Rev.* 14:11)

Some people cannot reconcile a loving God with eternal torment. Even many believers are so uncomfortable with hell that they try not to think of it at all. But as author Leslie Schmucker writes, "If we don't accept the reality of hell, we won't rightly understand the glory of the gospel."[1]

As we saw in question 13, those who reject Jesus will be "thrown into the lake of fire" at the final judgment (Rev. 20:15). Jesus, who spoke about hell more than anyone else in the entire Bible, referred to it as "Gehenna," which was a place outside Jerusalem where corpses and garbage rotted and burned. Jesus described hell as a place where the soul and the body are destroyed (see Matt. 10:28) and insisted, albeit hyperbolically, that it is better to gouge out your eye than to enter hell, where "the fire is not quenched" (Mark 9:47). New Testament writers described hell as a place of "gloomy darkness" (Jude 6), anguish, and torment (see Luke 16:19–31). While theologians debate if the fire and darkness are literal or symbolic, it is clear that hell is a place of ongoing, eternal misery (see Rev. 14:11; 2 Thess. 1:9).

How do we address those who think that a loving God would not allow unbelievers to be tortured? Only with great humility and full recognition of our blindness to the depth of our own sin. In that blindness, we don't fully grasp the darkness of sinful rebellion, and we don't fully grasp the holiness and goodness of God. As we begin to grapple with sin's darkness and God's holiness, we see that hell is a natural consequence of a commitment to live life apart from God. As Tim Keller notes, "People only get in the afterlife what they have most wanted—either to have God as Savior and Master or to be their own Saviors and Masters."[2]

As we consider the horror of hell and of our own sin, we again see the depth of God's love for us in Jesus Christ. On the cross, Jesus endured the torment of hell—he was forsaken by his Father so that we might be reconciled to God and adopted as his children. This is the love of our God: he sent his Son to earth as a human being, and this Son endured unspeakable agony, submitting to the death we deserved, so that his people might never suffer the horror of hell. This is the glorious message of the gospel.

> Let us love our God supremely,
> let us love each other too;
> let us love and pray for sinners,
> till our God makes all things new.
> **George Askins**

PRAYER

Holy Father, we confess that hell scares us—and that's a good thing. In our fear, help us to believe what your Word tells us about hell, so that we may treasure the good news of your saving grace and so that we may humbly and persistently urge others to turn from their sins, escape eternal torment, and take refuge in you. In Jesus's name, amen.

FURTHER ENCOURAGEMENT

Read Matthew 25:41–46; Mark 9:43–48; Luke 16:19–31; Revelation 14:11.
Read "The Uncomfortable Subject Jesus Addressed More than Anyone Else" by Leslie Schmucker.

FOR REFLECTION

What questions do you have about hell? Pray about them and discuss them with a fellow believer, especially a pastor or a ministry leader.

Part Three

Aging, Sickness, and Dying

Is there an "art" to dying?

O Lord, make me know my end and what is the measure of my days; let me know how fleeting I am! (*Ps.* 39:4)

In the fifteenth century, if you had walked into a local bookstore, you would have found a whole genre of literature filed under the section *ars moriendi*, which in Latin means "the art of dying." These pamphlets and booklets instructed people on how to die well. In journeying through this book, you are learning this very art.

Physician L. S. Dugdale insists that to die well, we must recover a "sense of finitude,"[1] the understanding that our "days [are] a few handbreadths" (Ps. 39:5). Dugdale also encourages us to embrace community and to resist the temptation to see the hospital as the "destination for dying,"[2] as many people do. As she points out, modern medicine has its limitations, among them, the inability to offer the dying the comforts of home, and we would do well to respect them.

> While I draw this fleeting breath,
> when mine eyelids close in death,
> when I soar to worlds unknown,
> see thee on thy judgment throne,
> Rock of ages, cleft for me,
> let me hide myself in thee!
> **Augustus M. Toplady**

J. Todd Billings, a theologian and author who himself lives with a terminal diagnosis, encourages us to rediscover the value of preparing for death as a lifelong feature of discipleship. He calls us to visit the sick, comfort the dying, and attend funerals. Like Dugdale, he urges us to recognize our mortality as we engage in daily activities such as eating, drinking, and playing. Billings notes, "Recognizing our mortal limits can lighten our load and deepen our joy."[3]

Allen Verhey, another theologian who wrote with a terminal diagnosis, encouraged readers to "commend life"—meaning we ought to value it—because it "belong[s] to the creative and redemptive cause of God."[4] Even as we commend life, we also recognize that following Jesus in a fallen world will eventually mean letting go of this life. Because resurrection and final restoration mean that death is not the end of the story for those who trust in Jesus, we can both commend life and accept aging and death.

Finally, to learn how to die well, we pay attention to how Jesus died. By studying Jesus's dying and death, we learn many things that prepare us to die well, like forgiving and seeking forgiveness (although Jesus, of course, did not need to seek forgiveness) (see Luke 23:34), leaving instructions for loved ones (see John 13–17), praying (see John 17), and acknowledging our bodies' needs (see John 12:1–8; 19:28). We also discover the virtues Jesus imparts to us through the Holy Spirit, virtues that help us face death: faith, hope, love, patience, humility, surrender, generosity, and courage.

Dear friend, when we remember that our lives are fleeting, we will prepare to die well; as we prepare to die well with the hope of glory, we will learn to live well.

PRAYER

Heavenly Father, may we have the courage to face our mortality, the wisdom to prepare to die well, and the faith, hope, and love in Christ to do so. In Jesus's name, amen.

FURTHER ENCOURAGEMENT

Read Psalm 39; Matthew 16:24–28; Luke 23:34.
Listen to "The Lost Art of Dying" with Lydia Dugdale.

FOR REFLECTION

Have you witnessed people who "died well"? What aspects of their approach to death would you like to adopt?

16

What does the Bible teach about the losses of aging?

Gray hair is a crown of glory; it is gained in a righteous life.
(*Prov.* 16:31)

Transhumanist Zoltan Istvan believes that we shouldn't have to die; to share his "gospel," he drove around the United States in the "Immortality Bus," "a brown bus spray-painted to look like a coffin."[1] Biogerontologist Andrew Steele, in his 2021 book *Ageless: The New Science of Getting Older without Getting Old*, proposes "biological immortality,"[2] arguing that aging should be viewed as a disease that will one day be cured. Agelessness and immortality appeal to a culture that will do anything to disguise or deny the fact that we're all, minute by minute, day by day, getting older. As the saying goes, "getting old ain't for sissies"—it involves loss of physical strength and beauty, loss of loved ones, and loss of independence. And yet, as Christians, we must ask, is agelessness really God's plan for us?

In the Bible, aging is assumed: "Aging and dying were considered to be natural, expected, even providential processes that were ordained and guided by God rather than discrete chronological stages of human development."[3] Genesis 15:15 states that Abraham would be "buried in a good old age." Psalm 90:10 proclaims that our lives are fleeting: "The years of our life are seventy, or even by reason of strength eighty . . . they are soon gone, and we fly away." For this reason, we should "number our days" (v. 12), making the most of each one.

E'en down to old age,
all my people shall prove
my sovereign, eternal,
unchangeable love;
and when hoary hairs
shall their temples adorn,
like lambs they shall still
in my bosom be borne.
Author unknown

While the Bible assumes that aging is natural, it doesn't glamorize it. Ecclesiastes 12 portrays the losses of aging graphically, even dismally. Using poetic language and imagery, the author details many casualties of aging, including weak hands trembling, teeth falling out, eyesight dimming, fears worsening, and mourning and grief increasing (vv. 3, 5).

Despite this suffering and loss, aging does have benefits, according to Scripture. For example, it can lead us to anticipate our heavenly dwelling more eagerly: "We know that if the tent that is our earthly home is destroyed, we have a building from God, a house not made with hands, eternal in the heavens" (2 Cor. 5:1). Aging also brings honor—it is an honor to be aged, and the aged are to be honored. The fifth commandment promises that honoring your father and mother leads to a lengthy life (see Ex. 20:12). Members of the church are exhorted to encourage older men and women and to honor widows (see 1 Tim. 5:1–3). Jesus rebukes the Pharisees for failing to care well for their parents (see Mark

7:9–13). According to the Bible, ageism is unacceptable in God's eyes.

In a world that urges us to resist aging, we must recapture the biblical view of the subject. As we do so, we will learn how to number our days, that we may gain a heart of wisdom.

PRAYER

Immortal and ageless God, the antiaging current in our culture threatens to overwhelm us. Help us to view aging as you do: as part of your providential design for humans, as a process that leads us to long for heaven, and as a season that gives us the wisdom to prepare for glory. In Jesus's ancient name, amen.

FURTHER ENCOURAGEMENT

Read Proverbs 16:31; Ecclesiastes 12; 2 Corinthians 5:1–10.
Listen to "Finishing Well" by J. I. Packer.

FOR REFLECTION

How do you feel about aging? What messages have you received about aging, and how have they shaped your thinking?

17

What does it look like to live wisely and graciously as we age?

So teach us to number our days that we may get a heart of wisdom. (*Ps.* 90:12)

Theologian and author J. I. Packer became blind due to macular degeneration at age eighty-eight, but he continued to serve God faithfully until he died five years later. Packer lived as he wrote, encouraging people to see their final years as the "last lap": "The final sprint, so I urge, should be a sprint indeed."[1] When we embrace the reality of aging, including its suffering, we discover opportunities to bear fruit, to share the gospel, and to enjoy peace in the face of death.

Even the painful losses of aging—loss of independence, loss of health, loss of loved ones—can lead us to a deeper intimacy with the Christ who comforts us in our suffering: "As we share abundantly in Christ's sufferings, so through Christ we share abundantly in comfort too" (2 Cor. 1:5). Those who embrace rather than deny the grief of aging will find the comfort of Christ, who suffered physical torment and died on a cross to bring an end to suffering and death.

Embracing the limitations of aging can also lead us to a deeper dependence on Christ, who himself took on the weakness of humanity by becoming man (see Phil. 2:1–11). When we wake up with back pain or need help carrying the groceries, we can turn to Christ and to others for support. As we become even more rooted in our reliance on Christ and others, the Spirit bears fruit in us: wisdom, patience, kindness, and the foresight to prepare for glory.

We are neither released nor disqualified from our calling to share the gospel as we age—ideally, we ought to do so even more. Scripture abounds with stories of older people who shared their wisdom and led people to glorify God. Jethro mentors his son-in-law Moses (see Ex. 18:13–27); Moses in turn mentors Joshua (see Ex. 24:13; 32:17–19; 33:11); and Elizabeth encourages Mary (see Luke 1:39–45). Psalm 92:14 reminds us that the righteous "still bear fruit in old age; they are ever full of sap and green."

> Haste thee on from grace to glory,
> arm'd by faith and wing'd by pray'r.
> Heav'n's eternal day's before thee;
> God's own hand shall guide thee there.
> Soon shall close this earthly mission;
> soon shall pass thy pilgrim days;
> hope shall change to glad fruition,
> faith to sight, and pray'r to praise.
> **Henry F. Lyte**

When we number our days, embracing aging and mortality, we will enjoy greater peace as death approaches. Because we have the hope of immortality, pastor Sam Allberry writes, "The signs of aging are no longer a threat but a promise. Gray hair and deepening lines on my face don't need to speak to me of a past that I can't recover but of a future I can barely conceive. The real glory days are not behind but ahead."[2]

Dear friend, we can embrace even the losses of aging with hope, knowing that aging moves us ever closer to the joy of eternal glory.

PRAYER

Everlasting God, help us to trust that you will work through our aging to reveal your glory and to prepare us for glory. May we number our days as we grow old and wise. In the name of our wise Savior, amen.

FURTHER ENCOURAGEMENT

Read Psalm 90:1–17.
Watch "Aging with Grace: The Back Story" with Karen Hodge, Susan Hunt, and Sharon Betters.

FOR REFLECTION

Think of some older believers you know. How have the losses of aging helped them to minister fruitfully to others?

18

What do sickness and death say about the strength of our faith?

Rabbi, who sinned, this man or his parents, that he was born blind? (*John* 9:2)

Kate Bowler, a Christian historian, conducted extensive research on American prosperity theology before she was diagnosed with terminal colon cancer. She observed that the false teaching of the prosperity gospel can deepen suffering in the face of sickness and the process of dying: "If a believer gets sick and dies, shame compounds the grief. Those who are loved and lost are just that—those who have lost the test of faith."[1] Many refuse to accept the reality of death: "An emaciated man was pushed about a megachurch in a wheelchair as churchgoers declared that he was already healed. A woman danced around her sister's deathbed shouting to horrified family members that the body can yet live. There is no graceful death, no *ars moriendi*, in the prosperity gospel."[2]

Although we may not buy into the prosperity gospel's false claims that God grants health and wealth based on a person's strong faith or lack of sin, we will frequently encounter its proponents when we face sickness and dying. For this reason, we need to have a sound biblical understanding of the relationship between faith and physical suffering.

As we saw in question 1, dying, death, and sickness resulted from the fall. However, we cannot correlate all death and sickness directly to individual sin. Jesus helps us to understand this when his disciples ask him about the cause of a man's blindness. The disciples assume that either the blind man or his parents sinned. Jesus tells them, "It was not that this man sinned, or his parents, but that the works of God might be displayed in him" (John 9:3). In other words, God sometimes allows us to fall ill so that he might display his glory. Jesus heals the blind man not to reward the man's faithfulness but to reveal his authority to those with eyes to see.

God does not always explain why people suffer and die. Job suffers the loss of his children, his livelihood, and his health without ever learning why. Paul tells us that God did not relieve him of a "thorn . . . in the flesh"—an unspecified physical malady—despite his persistent prayer for healing (2 Cor. 12:7). In the face of sickness and dying, we can learn to ask, "Where is God in this situation? How may his glory ultimately shine through this?"[3] Although we can pray for healing and seek God's wisdom when we and our loved ones are sick or dying, we can also rest in his sovereignty, knowing that healing does not depend on the strength of our faith or the degree of our holiness.

In our weary hours of sickness,
in our times of grief and pain,
when we feel our mortal weakness,
when the creature's help is vain,
by thy mercy, O deliver us, good Lord.
James J. Cummins

We can endure the suffering of sickness and dying because we know that full healing awaits us in glory.

PRAYER

Lord Jesus, thank you for freeing us from the shame of sickness and dying. Give us the faith to trust in your perfect timing and your perfect provision. In your name, amen.

FURTHER ENCOURAGEMENT

Read John 9:1–41.
Read "If We Prayed More Would Fewer of Our People Get Sick?" by Paul Carter.

FOR REFLECTION

Have you ever been made to think that an illness you had was connected to your lack of faith or your sinfulness? How would you respond if someone told you to pray harder so that you or a loved one could be healed?

19

How do we know which medical means to employ at the end of life?

Nor is he served by human hands, as though he needed anything, since he himself gives to all mankind life and breath and everything. (*Acts* 17:25)

You may have seen it in a show or a movie. A hospital patient's heart stops. Monitors show a flat line and beep loudly. Doctors and nurses rush to the patient's room; one yells, "Clear!" and another shocks the heart. Just like that, the patient is cured. There's no blood. No fractured ribs. No moving the patient to the ICU. No placing the patient on a mechanical ventilator. And no death, as there would be in about 90 percent of cases in which CPR is performed in the hospital.[1] CPR is just one of many end-of-life medical measures that is messier in real life than on TV.

As Christians who believe that God is completely sovereign over life and death, we need to gain wisdom about medicalized dying, in which "death is regarded as the great enemy to be defeated by the greater powers of science and

Father, I know that all my life
is portioned out for me;
the changes that are sure to come,
I do not fear to see:
I ask thee for a present mind,
intent on pleasing thee.
Anna L. Waring

medicine."[2] A recent Harvard study revealed that those who call themselves religious are most likely to seek aggressive end-of-life measures—some claim that they want to give God a chance to work a miracle.[3] As L. S. Dugdale, a physician and author, observes, "It seems curious that the people who believe most fervently in divine healing cling most doggedly to the technology of mortals."[4] May it not be so.

As we educate ourselves about end-of-life measures, we can better understand when they will sustain life and when they will prolong death. Bill Davis, a Christian philosopher and hospital ethics board consultant, teaches us how to apply biblical principles to various kinds of end-of-life medicine—CPR, ventilators, artificial nutrition, chemotherapy, and more—in his insightful book, *Departing in Peace: Biblical Decision-Making and the End of Life*. He notes, "While the Lord has blessed us with medical advances to combat death, their efficacy depends on his mercy. He does not need our help, nor does he call us to pursue futile interventions to give him time."[5]

Kathryn Butler, a critical care physician, reminds us that God has written his dignity into the very being and body of every human (see Gen. 1:26), and he alone determines our days (see Acts 17:25). When we must make decisions about which end-of-life measures to choose, we do not always have to accept all available medical measures, especially if they would cause significant suffering without enhancing quality or length of life. Because Christ has defeated death, we need not make life on earth the ultimate good. Remembering this helps us maintain perspective in the face of doctors whose primary goal may be to extend life on earth, no matter the cost.

As we prepare for glory, we must seek biblical wisdom, educate ourselves about end-of-life measures, and express our wishes in advance directives. In this way, we can show our willingness to trust God in life and in death.

PRAYER

Sovereign Lord, we confess that, at times, we look to medicine rather than to you for salvation. Give us the wisdom and the education we need to choose medical measures wisely and in a way that glorifies you. In the name of the One who heals us, amen.

FURTHER ENCOURAGEMENT

Read Genesis 9:1–7; 50:25; Psalm 90:12; Colossians 4:10.
Listen to "A Godly Perspective on End-of-Life Decisions" with Kathryn Butler.

FOR REFLECTION

What struggles have you and others you know experienced with various health-care options? What biblical principles would help you navigate these options?

Part Four

Living, Preparing, and Sharing Our Legacy

20

What information and documents do we need to gather to prepare our loved ones for our incapacitation or death?

Then Joseph made the sons of Israel swear, saying, "God will surely visit you, and you shall carry up my bones from here." (*Gen.* 50:25)

Unlike Joseph, who told his entire community what to do with his body (see Gen. 50:24–25), my father never shared his end-of-life wishes, despite knowing for two years that he was dying. I eventually worked up the courage to ask him to complete an advance directive, but because he so clearly didn't want to discuss his end-of-life wishes, I never asked him for details that would help us *after* his death.

As Christians who number our days, we can love our families well by preparing what I call a "practical legacy": the details that will help our loved ones when we are with Jesus. In this reading, we will discuss five important steps in preparing such a legacy, and in the next two reflections, we will explore funerals and wishes regarding the arrangements for our bodies.

Prepare an advance directive. An advance directive helps to guide health-care decisions in the case of incapacitation. It allows us to appoint a health-care proxy or a surrogate and to indicate what kind of treatment we would choose or decline in a medical crisis. As Bill Davis explains, “Legally executed advance directives diminish the burdens of fear and indecision from all those who will have to make medical decisions for us if we cannot make them ourselves.”[1]

Appoint a durable power of attorney. A durable power of attorney gives another person the legal authority to act on our behalf if we are incapacitated. If we are hospitalized or incapacitated, a person with the power of attorney will be able to pay bills and execute financial actions for us, such as close a bank account, trade stocks, or sign a contract. Some give the power of attorney to their health-care proxy, while others appoint different people for the two roles.

Could we but climb
where Moses stood
and view the landscape o'er,
not Jordan's stream,
nor death's cold flood,
should fright us from the shore.
Isaac Watts

Create a will and appoint an executor. Even if we have very little property, it is imperative that we make a will and appoint executors to handle our affairs after we die. Making a will is a way to steward the resources God has given us. It also clarifies our wishes regarding property distribution to our loved ones.

Organize and share passwords. Because our phones and other technological devices hold valuable, confidential information, it's essential to secure them with a password and to share that password with one trusted person. Additionally, we would be wise to gather our digital passwords in one secure location and to share that location with several trusted people.

Gather other essential information. To help in the case of incapacitation or to handle affairs after our death, we need to gather details about our medical history, personal history, insurance, titles and deeds, credit cards, bills, methods of payment, and so on.

When my mother died, she left behind a filing cabinet full of essential information, with a folder labeled "Emergency" that had a cover sheet titled "What to do when I die." In my shock and grief at her unexpected death, her guidance was a treasured gift. Dear friend, because we have the hope of glory, we can courageously create such a gift for our loved ones.

PRAYER

Wise Father, give us the wisdom, the courage, and the discipline we need to gather the information that will bless our loved ones in their grief. In Jesus's sufficient name, amen.

FURTHER ENCOURAGEMENT

Read Genesis 50:22–26; Matthew 25:14–30.

Listen to "Organizing Your Life and Legacy" with Elizabeth Turnage and Sharon Betters.

FOR REFLECTION

Have you created a practical legacy? If not, what has prevented you from doing so? Pray about it and ask a friend for encouragement and accountability.

21

What arrangements should we make for our bodies after our death?

For you are dust, and to dust you will return. (Gen. 3:19)

I'll never forget the day when I opened my front door and found a white 24-by-18-inch box neatly placed on my welcome mat. On the top and the side of the box were large orange stickers with the word *cremains* printed in white block letters. As disorienting as it was to see my mother's remains on my doorstep, I was deeply grateful that I'd not had to decide what to do with her body when she died unexpectedly. She had made arrangements with the crematory several years beforehand. Making decisions in advance about our wishes for our bodies after death will bring peace to our loved ones in the future.

As we consider these decisions, we need to remember two key biblical principles: first, God created us in his image; we are called to steward and honor our bodies because of

> Living or dying, Lord,
> I ask but to be thine;
> my life in thee, thy life in me,
> makes heav'n forever mine.
> **Henry Harbaugh**

the dignity he has given them. Second, our bodies need not be "intact" to be raised from the dead. Many Christians have rejected organ donation or cremation out of concern about the effect these procedures would have on their resurrection bodies. And yet, the Bible tells us that our bodies will return to dust (see Gen. 3:19), whether through burial or cremation, and that they will be raised as restored bodies when Jesus returns (see 1 Cor. 15:35–49; 1 Thess. 4:16). Keeping these principles in mind, we can make wise decisions about the disposition of our bodies.

First, we must decide about organ or body donation, which are matters of personal conviction to consider prayerfully. Organ donation can offer life to others when our lives have ended. Body donation to a medical school or a research facility provides students and researchers with opportunities to learn more about the body. The primary guiding principle behind organ and body donation is that our bodies are a gift from God to be stewarded wisely. If we do choose to donate our organs or our bodies, we must discuss our wishes with our families. Sadly, a would-be donor's plans are often ignored because the family refuses to comply or is unaware of them.

The next decision we need to make is whether to be cremated or buried. Although there aren't many references to cremation in Scripture, we do know that the bodies of Saul and his sons were cremated (see 1 Sam. 31:11–13). Cremation isn't against biblical counsel, but many theologians and pastors recommend burial because they believe it more clearly honors the dignity of the body. As Pastor Russell

Moore explains, "In burial, we're reminded that the body is not a shell, a husk tossed aside by the 'real' person, the soul within."[1]

Although some Christians may prefer burial for this reason, many theologians agree that both burial and cremation are biblically acceptable options. Because the cost of cremation is generally lower than that of burial, cremation may be a financially wise choice if funds are limited.

After we die, one of the first questions our loved ones will be asked is what they want to be done with our bodies. Communicating the answer to that question, and making arrangements in advance when possible, will bless our loved ones with profound peace in the midst of their grief.

PRAYER

Victorious Jesus, because you have defeated death, we can consider the hard realities that face our loved ones after we die. Guide us with your wisdom as we plan for the disposition of our bodies. In your comforting name, amen.

FURTHER ENCOURAGEMENT

Read 1 Corinthians 15:35–49; 2 Corinthians 5:7; 2 Timothy 4:7.
Read "The FAQs: What Christians Should Know about Cremation" by Joe Carter.

FOR REFLECTION

Have you ever thought about whether you want to be buried or cremated? What have you learned from others who have made their decisions about final arrangements in advance?

22

What kind of end-of-life service should we have?

It is better to go to the house of mourning than to go to the house of feasting, for this is the end of all mankind, and the living will lay it to heart. (*Eccl.* 7:2)

A fantasy-football-themed funeral? A family gathering at the eighteenth green of the golf course? An ice-cream truck that dispenses popsicles at the gravesite? You may have heard of such end-of-life services—perhaps you have even attended one. As early as 2006, journalist John Leland was writing about consumerist trends in end-of-life planning. Leland quotes funeral director Mark Duffey, who explains this trend: "Baby boomers are all about being in control. This generation wants to control everything, from the food to the words to the order of the service. And this is one area where consumers feel out of control."[1]

As we consider death with the hope of heaven, we must ask to what extent we should control our end-of-life services, and what principles should guide our planning.

Christians have the advantage of seeking counsel from pastors and other ministry leaders. Under their guidance, we can express wishes about Scripture readings, worship music, and receptions. We can also bless our loved ones by setting aside money for the cost of our services. While we plan, we should consider what makes for a "good funeral."

From a Christian perspective, a good funeral contains several key elements. A good funeral leads those present to mourn the curse of death and to face their own mortality. A good funeral also leads them to rejoice in the hope of glory: the saints enjoying God's loving presence. A good funeral typically celebrates the redemption stories of the deceased, remembering the unique gifts they had and the joy they brought others. A good funeral helps those present to grieve their loss. And a good funeral, above all, offers the hope of the gospel.

When my last hour cometh,
fraught with strife and pain,
when my dust returneth
to the dust again;
on thy truth relying
through that mortal strife,
Jesus, take me, dying,
to eternal life.
James Montgomery

Widow Clarissa Moll shows us how planning a good funeral can comfort loved ones in their grief. Clarissa's husband, Rob, a journalist, worked as a volunteer chaplain in hospice care as he researched his book, *The Art of Dying*. As he helped dying people to express their end-of-life wishes, he became convinced that he and Clarissa should make their own end-of-life plans. Though Clarissa resisted at first (they were only in their mid-thirties at the time), Rob eventually convinced her of the importance of facing their mortality. They began discussing advance directives, insurance, the disposition of their bodies, and funeral wishes.

When Rob died in a hiking accident at age forty-one, Clarissa, though numbed by the shock of his sudden death, found comfort in knowing Rob's wishes for his funeral. She writes, "The redemptive story told in the congregation of believers would carry me toward hope. . . . Rather than push death into the shadows, we grieved and worshiped in the light of eternal truth that day as we committed his body to the ground and his soul to God. Just as Rob had desired, in funeral worship, not his own story but the grand narrative of redemption with all of its tragedy and hope took center stage."[2]

Dear friend, because we have the hope of glory, we can do the hard things. Why not take some time today to pray over and plan for your funeral?

PRAYER

Heavenly Father, we confess our tendency to avoid talking about death. Give us the courage to plan end-of-life services that name the curse of death and affirm your grace to the grieving. Help us to plan end-of-life services that honor you above all and offer the hope of heaven to all who attend. In Jesus's name, amen.

FURTHER ENCOURAGEMENT

Read Ecclesiastes 7:2; 1 Thessalonians 4:13–18; Revelation 14:13. **Read** "Please Don't Make My Funeral All about Me" by Nancy Guthrie.

FOR REFLECTION

Have you ever considered planning your end-of-life service? Pray about how you would like to see God's story of grace told at this service.

23

What does the Bible say about stewarding our financial legacy?

As each has received a gift, use it to serve one another, as good stewards of God's varied grace. (1 *Peter* 4:10)

Although my dad knew he was dying for two years, he never made a will. I think his reasons were twofold: first, making a will would have required him to face the reality of his impending death, and second, he did not believe he had significant assets. My dad is not alone. Many people put off making a will. The truth is, whether we have a lot or a little, expressing our wishes for how others distribute our assets is not only a kindness to our loved ones—it is also a key principle of financial stewardship. As Christians, we can learn how to steward our financial legacy by considering what the Bible says about wealth and giving.

The book of Proverbs provides wisdom regarding wealth and poverty. From it, we learn that wealth can distract people

Goodness and mercy all my life
shall surely follow me:
and in God's house forevermore
my dwelling place shall be.
Francis Rous

from trusting the Lord (see Prov. 30:7-9). We also see that hard work is important, but we should not allow wealth to become our central focus (see Prov. 23:4-5). According to Proverbs, those who are wealthy should be generous to the poor (see Prov. 28:27) and should give generously to God out of gratitude for his sustenance (see Prov. 3:9).[1]

Elsewhere in Scripture, we learn more about financial stewardship. We should give sacrificially: Jesus praises the widow who gave a mite (the equivalent of about one-eighth of a penny), because she gave much out of her poverty (see Mark 12:41–44). We should give cheerfully: in 2 Corinthians, Paul says that "God loves a cheerful giver" (9:7). Both sacrificial and cheerful giving follow from God's love for us, as Eugene Peterson wrote: "There is no higher motive for Christian giving than the example God set for us when he gave his only Son. . . . The only way we're going to give delightfully is out of love."[2]

Because God has given to us so generously, we can joyfully plan how to distribute our possessions to bless future generations. To create our financial legacy, we might follow the five steps below.

Minimize debt. To relieve the burden for future generations, address debt now.

Take inventory of your assets and plan for distribution. Name beneficiaries for life insurance and IRAs. Consider all types of assets, including vehicles, jewelry, and valuable household items.

Consider consulting an estate attorney. Because tax law is complicated, estate attorneys can be helpful, even for small estates.[3]

Discuss your wishes with family. Whether you consult an attorney or not, communicating your wishes clearly will help to prevent future conflict.

Consider charitable giving. Tax consultant Adam Zylstra notes, "Some assets, like IRA accounts, are income taxable when received by an individual but pass free of income tax to charities. Your gifts can be structured to minimize tax and maximize the amount passing to both family and charity."[4]

In eternal glory, we will receive our full spiritual inheritance, "an inheritance that is imperishable, undefiled, and unfading" (1 Peter 1:4). Even if we have very little material wealth, we can leave a legacy of wise financial stewardship. As we address debt, become cheerful givers, and complete our will, we leave behind a financial and spiritual legacy that honors our generous God.

PRAYER

Gracious Father, how generously you have provided for all our needs. Because you have done so, we can loosen our grip on the gifts you have bestowed. Help us to steward our material wealth wisely. In Jesus's generous name, amen.

FURTHER ENCOURAGEMENT

Read Proverbs 30:7–9; 23:4–5; 3:9; 2 Corinthians 9:7; 1 Peter 1:3–5. **Read** "Giving When You're Gone" by Adam Zylstra.

FOR REFLECTION

What struggles have you experienced or seen others experience when the financial wishes of a dying person were not clearly expressed? What struggles do you have with your own financial legacy? Ask the Lord for wisdom and help in this area.

24

How do we let go of all the "stuff" we have accumulated?

Do not lay up for yourselves treasures on earth, where moth and rust destroy and where thieves break in and steal, but lay up for yourselves treasures in heaven, where neither moth nor rust destroys and where thieves do not break in and steal. (Matt. 6:19)

We've all heard the saying, "One person's trash is another person's treasure." The reverse can be true as well, particularly when it comes to a lifetime of accumulated possessions: one person's treasure can become another person's trash. Even though we may value our possessions, we must consider letting go as we prepare for eternal glory, releasing our hold on some of the "treasures on earth" to which we cling.

> Fading are the worldling's pleasures,
> all his boasted pomp and show;
> solid joys and lasting treasure
> none but Zion's children know.
> **John Newton**

Jesus urged his followers to store up treasures in heaven. He knew that too many possessions can clutter our minds and hearts, distracting our focus from our truest treasure: Jesus and the eternity we will spend with him. When we let go of possessions now—"giving with a warm hand rather than a cold one," as one friend says—we gain much. As we prepare for glory, we will find four benefits in letting go of some of our possessions:

Letting go can bring joy and satisfaction. It can be painful to part with objects that connect us to sweet memories, and we need not let go of all of them. But when we pass on books we'll never read again, clothes we'll never wear again, or equipment we'll never use again, we reap the joy of knowing that others will benefit from these things.

Letting go helps us to focus on the "treasures of heaven" and to be content with less. Not only will we reap the reward of moving more freely through our physical space, but we will also discover the freedom of a simpler life. We live in a consumeristic culture that breeds discontent. Learning to live with less is the surprising route to greater contentment.

Letting go of things now prepares us for the day when we will let go of our lives on this earth to live with Jesus eternally. Spiritual director Adele Calhoun observes, "The practice of letting go and embracing simplicity is one way we prepare ourselves for what is to come. Learning to live simply prepares us for our last breath while cultivating in us the freedom to truly live here and now."[1]

Letting go is a way to bless our loved ones after we're gone. One day, we will be with Jesus, and someone else will be left to decide what to do with our possessions. We can leave a holy blessing—a gift of treasures and stories and, yes, money—or an unholy mess—a mountain of dusty toilet paper and expired tomato soup, broken fishing rods, and dilapidated dining chairs. Which will it be?

To prepare for glory is to practice the spiritual discipline of donating or discarding some possessions and organizing what we keep. In so doing, we prepare a legacy that will bless our loved ones in their season of grief.

PRAYER

Generous Lord, free us from any possessions that would prevent us from truly treasuring you. Give us the courage to let go, that we might enjoy greater contentment and peace now. In Jesus's treasured name, amen.

FURTHER ENCOURAGEMENT

Read Matthew 5:37; 6:19–21; Philippians 4:11–12.
Read "Sentimental Items" by Becca Ehrlich.

FOR REFLECTION

Have you ever experienced joy in giving away a treasured possession? Have you ever received another person's treasured possession? How did that make you feel?

25

What is a spiritual legacy, and how do we create one?

We will not hide them from their children, but tell to the coming generation the glorious deeds of the LORD, and his might, and the wonders that he has done. (*Ps.* 78:4)

In Psalm 78, Asaph called the Israelites to remember and recount the wonders God had done for his people so that future generations would grow in faith, hope, and love. In short, he encouraged them to pass on their spiritual legacy.

To pass on my spiritual legacy, I will one day tell my grandchildren the story of how the Lord came to an unchurched fifteen-year-old girl who desperately needed the hope of God but didn't yet know it. I will tell them stories of playing tag football in the park as a ten-year-old, of meeting my husband in a college biology lab during one of the loneliest seasons of my life, of giving birth to precious children who became their precious parents. As I share these stories, they will see a thread, the bright scarlet thread of redemption that God has sewn through the tapestry of my life. They will see that thread running through their stories, too, binding them together, to God, to their family, and to a world aching for good news.

As we age, it is our privilege and our duty to share a spiritual legacy with future generations: stories, expertise, blessings, and wisdom. As we pass on this legacy, the next generation grows in faith, hope, and love. Let's consider some of the ways we can leave a spiritual legacy.

Pass on expertise or a skill. A counselor friend of mine passes along the tools and techniques she has refined over the years to younger counselors so that they won't have to learn these things the hard way. My grandmother shared the recipe for her famous yeast rolls, and with it her gift of hospitality, of gathering friends and strangers to feast on delicious food.

Give a blessing. Just as Isaac blessed Jacob before he died by telling him that nations would bow down to him (see Gen. 27:27–29), we can bless our loved ones by telling them how they uniquely reflect the image of God and how their gifts are serving the kingdom. Some people leave letters for family members or friends. Others regularly give these blessings during their lifetime, perhaps at birthday parties or on other special occasions.

Finish, then, thy new creation;
pure and spotless let us be:
let us see thy great salvation
perfectly restored in thee;
changed from glory into glory,
till in heav'n we take our place,
till we cast our crowns before thee,
lost in wonder, love, and praise.
Charles Wesley

Share stories, values, and wisdom. As Proverbs 20:15 tells us, "Wise words are more valuable than much gold and many rubies" (NLT). We long to pass on the wisdom that we have learned over a lifetime, in the way we live today as well as in stories and insight we leave for later.

It takes time, intentionality, and prayer to pass on the stories and lessons that point to God's "abundant goodness" (Ps. 145:7), but as we do so, we will strengthen our loved ones in faith, hope, and love.

PRAYER

Author God, you have written so many stories of redemption in our lives; you have given us so many good gifts of wisdom and knowledge. Give us the courage and discipline to share this legacy faithfully, that others might know your goodness. In the name of our wise Savior, amen.

FURTHER ENCOURAGEMENT

Read Psalm 145:1–7; 78:1–8; Proverbs 20:15.
Read "Sharing the Stories of Your Life: Why It's Important and How to Do It" by Elizabeth Turnage.

FOR REFLECTION

Set a timer for ten minutes and record a story or a life lesson that you would like to pass on to others. Make an appointment on your calendar to record more stories and lessons weekly or monthly.

26

What is an emotional legacy, and how do we leave one?

Having loved his own who were in the world, he loved them to the end. (*John* 13:1)

In his insightful book, *The Four Things That Matter Most*, Ira Byock, a palliative care physician, offers his "recommendations for mending, tending, and celebrating relationships" at the end of life: "Please forgive me. I forgive you. Thank you. I love you."[1] In the final chapter of the book, Byock adds a fifth task: saying goodbye. Attending to these tasks regularly, far before we approach the end of life, helps us to create an emotional legacy that imparts comfort, peace, and hope to our loved ones. United to Jesus, we find the courage to leave an emotional legacy that points others to Christ. In this meditation, we will consider how Jesus himself says "goodbye" and "I love you." In the next two meditations, we will consider forgiveness and gratitude.

Not only did Jesus express his love for his followers in his life and in his death, but he also communicated it to his disciples in the final words, deeds, and prayers of the Upper Room Discourse in John 13–17. Jesus served his disciples by washing their feet and instructed them to "wash one another's feet" (13:14). He exhorted them to love one another because he had first loved them (see v. 34). He promised them that he would not leave them alone, saying that he would send the Helper, the Holy Spirit (see 14:16). Finally, Jesus prayed for himself and for his disciples, that he would be glorified, that the Father would protect them, and that the Father would sanctify them (see 17:1, 5, 15, 17). Just as Jesus expressed his love for his followers, we can express our love by serving our loved ones, by urging them to love one another with Christ's love, by pointing them to their Comforter, the Holy Spirit, and by praying for and with them.

In his goodbye, Jesus left the instructions he knew his disciples would need in the coming days and years. He prepared them for suffering and reminded them of the faith that would help them endure: "Let not your hearts be troubled. Believe in God; believe also in me" (John 14:1). He reminded them of their purpose—to "do the works" that he does (v. 12)—and of their dependence on him to do those works (see 15:5). He left them the Spirit to "teach [them] all things" (14:26). He gave them hope, that they would one day be reunited with him in their heavenly home: "If I go and prepare a place for you, I will come again and will take you to myself, that where I am you may be also" (v. 3). He prayed "that they may become perfectly one" (17:23) and "that the love with which you have loved me may be in them" (v. 26). As we consider how to say goodbye to loved ones, we can

> My soul rejoices to pursue
> the steps of him I love,
> till glory breaks upon my view,
> in brighter worlds above.
> **William Cowper**

follow Jesus's lead by pointing them to the hope of heaven and by reminding them of their glorious purpose in Christ.

Dear friend, because we have the hope of glory, and because we are empowered by the love of Christ and helped by the Holy Spirit, we can say goodbye to our loved ones and leave a legacy of love.

PRAYER

Gracious God, we are deeply humbled by our Savior's final acts of love toward his disciples. As we look forward to his welcome in glory, may we bless our loved ones with faithful farewells. In Jesus's loving name, amen.

FURTHER ENCOURAGEMENT

Read John 13–17.
Read "Day 29" of *Abide in Me: 31 Days with Jesus and the Upper Room Discourse* by the Presbyterian Church in America's Committee on Discipleship Ministries.

FOR REFLECTION

Have you ever received an emotional legacy? How does learning about Jesus's farewell encourage you to accomplish one of the tasks mentioned?

27

How do we forgive and ask forgiveness as we near the end of life?

Be kind to one another, tenderhearted, forgiving one another, as God in Christ forgave you. (*Eph.* 4:32)

Near the end of my dad's life, I lost my temper with him. I had missed his last two oncology appointments because I had been in another city caring for our son as he recovered from surgeries to treat a brain tumor. Now I was back, and I found that my dad's condition had deteriorated—he required a wheelchair just to make it to the oncologist's office.

An hour into the wait, my patience was already running thin when my dad ever so casually mentioned that he had discontinued his oral chemotherapy treatment. I was angry—not because he had discontinued the treatment, but because when I had checked on him while I was out of town, he had told me that he was, in his words, "tip-top."

The woman sitting in the chair next to me observed my anger and my dad's embarrassment and spoke up: "It will all be okay." She paused briefly and said, "It will all be okay, as long as you know Jesus." I have always thought of that woman as the "angel in the waiting room." She reminded me of the truth I needed at that moment: because Jesus has forgiven our sins, and because of the hope of glory, it truly will "all be okay."

Knowing that we have been forgiven by Jesus, we can both ask for and extend forgiveness as we or others approach the end of life and the beginning of glory. In that awful waiting room moment, I needed to ask my earthly father's forgiveness, and I needed to remember my heavenly Father's forgiveness. Because of my heavenly Father's forgiveness, I could also extend forgiveness to my earthly father for hiding the truth of his condition from me.

Once the world's Redeemer, dying,
bore our sins upon the tree;
on that sacrifice relying,
now I look in hope to thee:
Father, take me; all forgiving,
fold me to thy loving breast;
in thy love forever living
I must be forever blest.
Ray Palmer

What does it mean to forgive? Let's begin with what forgiveness is not. It is not denying, excusing, or minimizing an offense. Rather, to forgive is to name the harm, first to ourselves and to God and sometimes to the offender. Forgiveness is a process that often takes time and that often benefits from the wise counsel of others. To forgive is to let go of our desire to make another person pay for their wrong against us and to pray for the offender's good (see Matt. 5:44). To forgive is to seek reconciliation while realizing that the person we are forgiving may be unable or unwilling to repent of their sin and to restore the relationship.

Similarly, to ask forgiveness is to name our offense against another without denying, excusing, minimizing, or blame-shifting. To ask forgiveness requires the humility and the clarity to see how we have harmed another and God. As we ask forgiveness, we seek to change our behavior through repentance, which is utterly dependent on the Holy Spirit's work in us.

For Christians, extending and asking forgiveness are regular rhythms of our lives. As we near the end of our lives, looking forward to the day in glory when we will know the full freedom of our forgiveness in Christ, it is only natural that we become more intentional about practicing forgiveness. In doing so, we have the opportunity to leave an emotional legacy that will bless others for years to come.

PRAYER

Forgiving Father, thank you for sending your Son to pay the unpayable debt of our sins against you. By dying on the cross, he reconciled us to you. Because we have been not only forgiven but also made righteous in Christ, help us to forgive and ask forgiveness of others. In Jesus's name, amen.

FURTHER ENCOURAGEMENT

Read Matthew 18:21–35; 5:43–45; Ephesians 1:7; 4:32.
Read "Tim Keller Wants to Help You Forgive" by Matt Smethurst.

FOR REFLECTION

Has anyone forgiven you, or intentionally withheld forgiveness, at the end of their life? If so, what did that mean to you? Do you need to seek or extend forgiveness to someone now? Pray that God would strengthen you and give you wisdom in this area.

28

Why is it important to express our gratitude as we or a loved one nears the end of life?

For it is all for your sake, so that as grace extends to more and more people it may increase thanksgiving, to the glory of God. (2 *Cor.* 4:15)

After her father suffered a massive stroke, journalist Katy Butler began writing him "legacy letters," letters thanking him for the kindness he had shown her throughout her life.[1] Legacy letters are just one of many ways we can intentionally express gratitude at the end of our lives.

For Christians, gratitude is the natural response to God's grace toward us. Although we may experience pain and suffering near the end of our lives, we also have the hope of glory and the assurance that God will one day restore all that is broken. For this reason, we can express gratitude even as we name our struggles and sorrows. In this, we follow the example of the apostle Paul, who wrote, "We are pressed on every side by troubles, but we are not crushed. We are perplexed, but not driven to despair. We are hunted down, but never abandoned by God" (2 Cor. 4:8–9 NLT). Paul thanked God even in the midst of his suffering because more people were discovering God's grace, and more people were glorifying God (see v. 15).

When this passing world is done,
when has sunk yon glaring sun,
when we stand with Christ in glory,
looking o'er life's finished story,
then, Lord, shall I fully know,
not till then, how much I owe.
Robert Murray McCheyne

Near the end of his life, Jesus demonstrated the importance of gratitude. When Mary of Bethany expressed gratitude to him by anointing him for burial, Jesus honored her for her loving act (see John 12:1–8). Before Jesus shared the Last Supper with his disciples, he gave thanks (see Matt. 26:27). Facing an agonizing death, Jesus could give thanks because he knew that he would soon be in glory with his Father and that he would soon accomplish his mission of reconciliation.

Because Christians are people of gratitude, we can be intentional about thanking the people in our lives, throughout our lives, as we and they approach the end. In *The Thank-You Project*, author Nancy Davis Kho wrote one thank-you letter each week, for fifty weeks, to fifty different recipients. Although she began by thanking people who had shown her kindness or had inspired her, she also included those whom she had previously considered enemies. As she wrote letters to her so-called enemies, she found herself forgiving them. Kho sometimes felt awkward about writing these letters, but as she saw the recipients' grateful responses, she felt compelled to continue.[2] We need not write letters to fifty people, and in the end stages of illness we may not be able to do so, but we can find simple ways to express gratitude, with calls or texts or hugs.

Dear friend, grace leads to gratitude. As those who will one day experience deeper gratitude than we've ever known when we meet God in glory, we have every reason to express gratitude to those who have been instruments of God's redemptive work in our lives on earth. Let's not wait. Let's start building a legacy of gratitude today.

PRAYER

Gracious God, how thankful we are for your goodness in our lives! Help us to thank those who have shown us your grace and those who have shaped us in other ways. In Jesus's name, amen.

FURTHER ENCOURAGEMENT

Read Matthew 26:27; John 12:1–8; 2 Corinthians 4:7–18.
Read "The Thank-You Project," an interview of Nancy Davis Kho by Nicole Lutze.

FOR REFLECTION

Has anyone ever expressed gratitude to you near the end of their life? How did that make you feel? How might you build a legacy of gratitude as you prepare for glory?

Part Five

The Church and Preparing for Glory

29

How does being part of a church help us to care for the sick and dying?

And the King will answer them, "Truly, I say to you, as you did it to one of the least of these my brothers and sisters, you did it to me." (*Matt.* 25:40)

According to L. S. Dugdale, when medical personnel cannot locate the family or friends of dying patients, they describe these patients as "unbefriended."[1] We are called to care for "the least of these," so we long to ensure that no one is ever left to die alone. As we offer compassionate care to the sick and dying, we prepare for eternal glory by becoming more like Christ, by remembering our own mortality, and by speaking and hearing last and lasting words.

While our culture tends to isolate the sick and dying as if death is contagious, Jesus teaches us to serve "the least of these." In Matthew 25, he used a parable to describe how he will distinguish believers from unbelievers on judgment day:

believers are those who cared for him when he was hungry, thirsty, homeless, naked, sick, or imprisoned. How did they do this? Jesus says, "Truly, I say to you, as you did it to one of the least of these my brothers and sisters, you did it to me." Although acts of compassion do not earn our place in eternal glory, they do demonstrate our faith in Christ and reveal that we are becoming more like him.

As we visit and care for the sick and dying, we remember our own mortality, and we learn to fear it less. Because we have the hope of eternal glory, we can offer a compassionate presence to the sick and dying. We can pat a person's hand and tell them we love them. We can sing for them. We can pray for them.

As we visit and care for dying loved ones, we also make space to pass on the last and lasting words of the emotional legacy we saw earlier. We offer or ask forgiveness, we thank the person for the ways they have blessed us, and we tell them we love them. We also invite them to share lasting words or wisdom with us. In these ways we wish them a gracious farewell.

Comfort, comfort ye my people,
speak ye peace, thus saith our God;
comfort those who sit in darkness,
mourning 'neath their sorrow's load.
Johannes Olearius

Although visiting and caring for the sick and dying are helpful ways to prepare for glory, they are often difficult for those who have past trauma related to hospitals, illness, or death. If you struggle with these things, consider other ways to show compassion to sick and dying loved ones. Make a meal, run errands, or offer childcare. Share your goodbyes by writing a letter or making a video call. The Christ who calls us to care for "the least of these" will care for you in these hard places and will guide you as you care for others.

As we serve our sick and dying loved ones, we anticipate the day when we will meet our compassionate, loving Shepherd and hear him say, "Well done, good and faithful servant" (Matt. 25:21).

PRAYER

Good Shepherd, help us to offer our compassionate presence to the sick and dying. Show us how to care for them, and please sustain us as we do so. In your tender name, amen.

FURTHER ENCOURAGEMENT

Read Matthew 25:31–46.
Read "Some Thoughts on Ministering to the Sick and Dying" by Kevin DeYoung.

FOR REFLECTION

If you have visited the sick and dying, what have you found beneficial about doing so? If you struggle with visiting the sick and dying, what other ways could you serve them?

30

How do we care for someone as they near death?

Standing by the cross of Jesus were his mother and his mother's sister, Mary the wife of Clopas, and Mary Magdalene.
(*John* 19:25)

Many of us have experienced the second-guessing that comes after a loved one dies: *Did I do enough? Why wasn't I there? How could I have kept them from suffering so much pain?* Others have known the profound joy of witnessing a believing loved one pass peacefully into their Savior's presence. How do we care for others in their final days and hours? First, we must be willing to face death with the hope of heaven. Equipped with that hope, we must then prayerfully seek wisdom regarding health-care decisions, offer spiritual care through fellowship and prayer, and remember to care for the caregiver.

When we know that death is not the end, we more easily shift our focus from cure to care. Emboldened by the hope of heaven, we find the courage and the wisdom to ask our doctors for a referral to hospice. Hospice is a program funded

> Oh, I must watch and pray
> for that blest hour no soul may know;
> and I would ever ready be
> for Jesus when he calleth me.
> **Flora H. Cassel**

by Medicare when a doctor believes a patient has six months or fewer to live. It provides a team of physicians, nurses, social workers, counselors, and chaplains, all of whom are equipped to care for dying patients. The team recognizes the physical signs of the patient's final days and hours, manages the pain that can accompany dying, and attends to the spiritual and practical needs of the dying person and their loved ones.

Whether or not we choose hospice, we ought to follow the lead of Jesus's family and friends who offered their compassionate presence as he died. We can pray for and with the person, praying all types of prayers: adoring our Father in heaven and praising Jesus for the gift of eternal life, confessing sins and fears and doubts, lamenting and grieving, thanking God for his many blessings, and asking him to care for our loved ones. As we listen and pray and ask appropriate questions, we can help our loved one build an emotional legacy by forgiving, asking forgiveness, and saying thank you, "I love you," and goodbye. (See questions 26, 27, and 28.) We can sing with and over the dying person, and we can ask for and listen to their stories.

Because Jesus is ever-present with us through the Holy Spirit, we can attend to the spiritual needs of the dying as they prepare to meet their Savior face to face.

PRAYER

Heavenly Father, we confess that we often fear being with the dying, confused as we are about what to do and say.

Help us to remember that in Christ, we have every resource we need to offer kind and comforting presence to a person in their final days and hours. In Jesus's comforting name, amen.

FURTHER ENCOURAGEMENT

Read John 19:16–27.
Listen to comforting music on Singing Christ's Hope into Suffering, Lauri Hogle's Youtube channel.

FOR REFLECTION

Have you ever been with a person as they died? If so, what was that experience like for you? If not, how do you feel about the possibility of doing so in the future?

31

How can we care for caregivers?

When Jesus saw her weeping . . . he was deeply moved in his spirit and greatly troubled. (*John* 11:33)

As we prepare for glory, we must follow Jesus's lead in offering comfort to caregivers, and if we are caregivers, we can reach out for and welcome the comfort of others.

Because caregiving can lead to anxiety, depression, fear, grief, guilt, shame, isolation, doubt, and poor health,[1] caregivers need our support. Although caregiving can also lead to joy and fulfillment, that joy only comes when caregivers find meaning in their suffering and receive the support of their communities.

> In sickness, sorrow, want, or care,
> whate'er it be, 'tis ours to share;
> may we where help is needed, there
> give help as unto thee.
> **Godfrey Thring**

To understand how to care for caregivers, let's observe Jesus's response to them in Scripture. With Martha, Jesus was tender but truthful. He gave her hope as she grieved the loss of her brother: "I am the resurrection and the life" (John 11:25).

With the brokenhearted Mary of Bethany, Jesus wept (see vv. 32–35). When Mary anointed his body before his death, Jesus honored her (see Matt. 26:10). As author and caregiver Marissa Bondurant writes, "In all your caregiving, Jesus is caring tenderly for you."[2]

We must follow Jesus's lead by offering practical and spiritual comfort to those who are caring for the sick and dying. Below are just a few of the ways we can join Jesus in caring for caregivers.

Pray for caregivers when we pray for the sick. Whenever possible, pray with the caregiver. Caregiving can lead to spiritual and emotional exhaustion; offering a prayer by phone or by text can soothe a frenzied heart and mind.

Listen for the spiritual and emotional struggles caregivers experience and affirm their grief. As we have seen, Jesus wept with Mary of Bethany. Avoid quick-fix answers to a caregiver's profound questions and deep concerns about their loved one's suffering. Instead, offer the presence of Christ with compassionate listening and gently point them to the Savior who grieved death and who died for them.

Urge caregivers to attend to their own health needs and offer respite care to them. Studies show that many caregivers suffer from serious health problems because they miss their own medical appointments. Remind caregivers you know that their own well-being is crucial and help them, as much as you are able, to attend to their own health.

Assist with practical needs. Whether it's mowing the lawn, paying bills, filing for insurance, buying groceries, cooking meals, or hanging Christmas lights, you can relieve a caregiver's burden by doing tasks that they have not the time, energy, or ability to do.

Dear friend, what better way to prepare for glory than to offer Jesus's care to those who care for the sick and dying?

PRAYER

Comforting Jesus, make us a comfort to those who care for the least of these. Give us the wisdom and the compassion to help our caregiving friends. In your loving name, amen.

FURTHER ENCOURAGEMENT

Read John 11.
Read "Gospel Comfort for Caregivers: Six Ways Your Church Can Help" by Elizabeth Turnage.

FOR REFLECTION

If you have been or currently are a caregiver, write down some of the helpful ways people have cared for you. If you haven't been a caregiver, ask a caregiver how people have ministered the love of Christ to them. If you have a caregiver, how can you care for them?

32

How do I care for myself as a caregiver?

Come to me, all who labor and are heavy laden, and I will give you rest. (*Matt.* 11:28)

When my father was dying of cancer, and I was caring for our twenty-two-year-old son, who had undergone three surgeries for a brain tumor, I neglected my health needs. I skipped my yearly physical and my yearly mammogram. I ate more sugar and exercised less. I slept poorly. Strands of hair came out in my hands as I washed it. Fatigue fell over me like a persistent fog. During my most intense season of caregiving, my care for myself deteriorated rapidly, and my body paid the price.

I was not alone. Unpaid caregivers have an earlier and higher mortality rate than non-caregivers as a result of neglecting their own physical health.[1] Caregivers must obey the call to steward their bodies well by making self-care a priority. How do we do so?

First, we recognize that it is not self-indulgent to care for our mental, emotional, spiritual, and physical well-being. When Jesus called us to deny ourselves, he didn't mean for us to deny or denigrate our humanity—our need for rest, exercise, good nutrition, and medical care. Jesus himself acknowledged his human limitations by sleeping, eating, and taking time away from his ministry to pray and rest (see Matt. 14:22–23; Mark 4:35–40). Jesus tended to his own and to others' physical needs, showing us how to "glorify God" in our bodies, which are the "temple of the Holy Spirit" (1 Cor. 6:20, 19).

Second, we must rely on the Holy Spirit to grow us in humility and dependence. Many caregivers harm their bodies by refusing to accept their physical limitations. My husband, an orthopedic surgeon, regularly sees patients who have torn a rotator cuff or fractured a hip while caring for a loved one. Caregivers must learn to "boast all the more gladly" in their weaknesses, believing that weakness is truly the gospel way (2 Cor. 12:9). As caregivers accept their limitations, they will humbly seek and receive the help offered by the body of Christ (see question 31).

Finally, we can turn away from self-sufficiency and trust in God to provide for our loved one's needs. One friend shared the story of refusing all offers of help after her husband had a stroke. She was afraid that no one else could care for her husband as well as she could, so she almost never left his side. After three weeks, my friend collapsed from exhaustion and was hospitalized. At this point, she realized that she had

There are depths of love
that I cannot know
till I cross the narrow sea;
there are heights of joy
that I may not reach
till I rest in peace with thee.
Fanny J. Crosby

not trusted God to care for her husband. Healthy self-care requires us to turn away from our sinful tendency toward self-sufficiency and to submit instead to the good plans of the Lord.

Caregivers enjoy a profound privilege as we tend to loved ones in their time of need. Nevertheless, we endure emotional, mental, and physical stress. As we learn to rest, exercise, eat well, fellowship, and get medical care, we accept Jesus's kind invitation: "Come to me, all who labor and are heavy laden, and I will give you rest" (Matt. 11:28).

PRAYER

Precious Jesus, you indeed beckon us to come to you for rest. Help all caregivers to hear and receive your invitation, trusting in you to care for their loved ones. In your rest-giving name, amen.

FURTHER ENCOURAGEMENT

Read 1 Corinthians 6:19; 2 Corinthians 12:8–10; Mark 4:35–40.
Read "How Jesus Cares for Caregivers" by Marissa Bondurant.

FOR REFLECTION

If you are a caregiver, have you accepted Jesus's invitation to rest? Why or why not? If you are not a caregiver, how can you encourage a caregiver to care for themselves?

33

How does participating in church prepare us for glory?

But you, beloved, building yourselves up in your most holy faith and praying in the Holy Spirit, keep yourselves in the love of God, waiting for the mercy of our Lord Jesus Christ that leads to eternal life. (*Jude* 20–21)

My pastor, Joel Treick, recently preached on death. Well, not simply death, but on the commandment, "You shall not murder" (Ex. 20:13). In his sermon, our pastor reminded us that the gospel teaches a twofold truth about human life: first, we should value life because God created it; second, we should know that life on this earth is not the ultimate good. Our pastor shared his own end-of-life wishes, as expressed in his advance directive, to "depart and be with Christ" (Phil. 1:23) rather than to prolong death with aggressive health-care measures.

As we heard the preaching of the Word, the members of my church were invited to prepare for glory by considering the gospel's implications for end-of-life wishes. Worship, baptism, and communion, among other aspects of church membership, also help us to prepare for glory.

In weekly worship, we gather (ideally) with people who are both like and unlike us—people with different political views, skin tones, vocations, and families. United by Christ, we pray, we affirm our beliefs, and we join our voices to sing of the glory and goodness of God. In doing so, we prepare for the day when we will gather to worship with people of every tribe and tongue and nation (see Rev. 7:9). Indeed, church worship is a foretaste of the glorious day when we will be perfected as the beautifully diverse yet wholly unified body of Christ.

> May thy gospel's joyful sound
> conquer sinners, comfort saints;
> may the fruits of grace abound,
> bring relief for all complaints.
> Thus let ev'ry Lord's Day prove,
> till we join the church above.
> **John Newton**

As we participate in or witness baptism, we are reminded of our spiritual death and resurrection: "We were buried therefore with him by baptism into death, in order that, just as Christ was raised from the dead by the glory of the Father, we too might walk in newness of life" (Rom. 6:4). Baptism reminds us that just as we have died and have been raised with Christ spiritually, we will one day die and be raised with Christ physically.

As we take communion, the Lord's Supper, we "proclaim the Lord's death until he comes" (1 Cor. 11:26). When we eat of the bread and drink from the cup, we remember that Christ fully paid for our sins. But we do so "until he comes," looking forward to the day when Christ will return. In that day, we will dine with him as his fully glorified bride at "the marriage supper of the Lamb" (Rev. 19:9).

Dear friend, participation in a local church leads us to "set [our] minds on things that are above" (Col. 3:2). As we pray and sing and grieve and baptize and take communion and hear the gospel preached, we remember the death and resurrection of the One who loves us fully. As we remember that death and resurrection, we are assured that we live as his new creation now, looking forward to the day when we will join him as his lovely bride in the new heavens and the new earth.

PRAYER

Heavenly Bridegroom, you have called the church to be your beautiful, glorified bride. Help us to participate in the joys of church today so that we might reflect on the eternal glory that we will enjoy forever. In your loving name, amen.

FURTHER ENCOURAGEMENT

Read Luke 22:14–20; Romans 6:1–14; Revelation 19:10.
Read "Martin Luther on Preparing to Die" by Stéphane Simonnin.

FOR REFLECTION

How has participation in a local church already helped you to prepare for eternal glory?

34

How does prayer prepare us for glory?

The Lord is at hand; do not be anxious about anything, but in everything by prayer and supplication with thanksgiving let your requests be made known to God. (*Phil.* 4:5–6)

Many of us know that prayer eases anxiety and brings peace that "surpasses all understanding" (Phil. 4:7), but we may not realize that a regular practice of prayer also prepares us to face sickness, dying, and death. Eric Tonjes, whose wife died of cancer, described how God soothed his soul as he confessed his fear about her diagnosis: "Nothing about our situation was changed, but my racing heart slowed as I beheld the one who was on the throne."[1]

> These are they whose hearts were riven,
> sore with woe and anguish tried,
> who in prayer full oft have striven
> with the God they glorified;
> now, their painful conflict o'er,
> God has bid them weep no more.
> **Heinrich T. Schenk**

Let's consider how the four aspects of the ACTS approach

to prayer—adoration, confession, thanksgiving, and supplication—prepare us for glory.

Adoration. As we adore God, sing his praises, and list all of his glorious attributes, we are reminded, as Tonjes was, that God is mighty, majestic, and merciful. The God who created the cosmos and our very bodies is the same God who determines the number of our days (see Ps. 39:5). As we praise God for his goodness, we remember his mercy in sending his very own Son to die that we might become his children, and we are led to trust him more readily in the face of death.

Confession. Michael Hoppe, a hospice chaplain, explains that dying patients often experience "existential pain"—pain due to regret or guilt.[2] Those who confess their sins daily may experience less existential pain because they regularly name their transgressions and ask God's forgiveness. Each day, as we pray, "Forgive us our debts as we also have forgiven our debtors" (Matt. 6:12), we are freed from the burden of guilt we might otherwise carry.

Thanksgiving. When we regularly thank God for our daily bread (see Matt. 6:11), for his forgiveness in Christ, and for his blessing of our friends and family and church, we remember that we were made to be dependent on God and interdependent on others. We may spend the first thousand years in eternal glory saying "thank you" to God as we see clearly how he has saved us and provided for us. Thanksgiving prepares us for the heavenly joys that await us.

Supplication. We regularly request that God would heal the sick and dying. As we do so, we begin to see how God's ways are beyond our ways, for sometimes he heals on this earth, and sometimes he heals by taking our loved one home to glory. Praying for others also readies us for eternal glory by making us more like Christ in our compassion, patience, and humility. Often, as we pray, we are moved to comfort others; in this way, God makes us the answer to our own prayers.

Dear friend, let us take comfort in the Lord's nearness. As we make prayer a regular daily practice, we anticipate the day in eternal glory when we will speak with the Lord face to face.

PRAYER

Heavenly Father, draw our hearts toward heaven as we adore you, confess our sins, thank you for your provision, and ask you for help. As we face the reality of death, give us your surpassing peace. In the name of Christ, amen.

FURTHER ENCOURAGEMENT

Read Matthew 6:5–15; Psalm 118. **Listen** to "The Valley of Vision: The Trinity" read by Max McLean.

FOR REFLECTION

In what ways can you see your prayers preparing you for eternal glory?

Part Six

The Journey of Grief

35

How can we cope with the physical, spiritual, and emotional impacts of grief?

He was despised and rejected by men, a man of sorrows and acquainted with grief. (Isa. 53:3)

All you want to do today is wrap yourself in a soft blanket and lose yourself in a mediocre book, but the fellowship committee you lead expects you at church at 11 a.m. to set up for the annual Christmas dinner. Did they forget that your spouse died four months ago? You drag yourself out of bed and get yourself dressed. You have become a person acquainted with grief.

And yet, there is hope, for you have a companion in your grief. His name is Jesus. Not only does he know your grief, but he has also borne your grief for you. He has suffered on your behalf so that, one day, you might never suffer again (see Isa. 53:3–4, 10). United to our compassionate Savior, we can navigate the sometimes turbulent journey of grief.

Be still, my soul:
when dearest friends depart,
and all is darkened
in the vale of tears,
then shalt thou better
know his love, his heart,
who comes to soothe
thy sorrow and thy fears.
Be still, my soul:
when change and tears are past
all safe and blessed
we shall meet at last.
Katharina von Schlegel

We can even learn to enjoy restful and peaceful days along the way.

Let's consider how Jesus helps us to endure the physical, emotional, and spiritual challenges of grief.

Grief affects us physically. It affects our appetite, our digestion, and our cravings. It drains us of energy and the desire to exercise. It interrupts our sleep and weakens our immune system. Because Jesus suffered in a human body, he understands physical suffering. Because Jesus is the Great Physician who cares for our bodies, we too must care for them. When needed, we must seek medical attention to address grief's physical impact on us.

Grief affects us emotionally. Disbelief, anger, sorrow, desperation, agitation. Peace, hope, joy. The emotions of grief refuse to be confined to five neat stages. Young widow Clarissa Moll counsels us to pay attention to our emotions: "Feel the sorrow deeply. Express the despair, the doubt, the anger, the exhaustion. And when you catch your breath, take a deep inhale of hope. Listen for the quiet whisper of possibility. Drink deeply the rich words of joy that Scripture offers you, not in isolation of your suffering but in its presence."[1]

Grief affects us spiritually. It is normal to ask why, especially after a shocking loss. As we will see in question 36, we can take refuge in the laments of Scripture, comforted by the awareness that Jesus himself lamented as he hung on the cross: "My God, my God, why have you forsaken me?" (Matt. 27:46). We persist in pleading honestly with the Lord to show us his mercy. We invite others to plead on our behalf when our hearts run dry. We take comfort in knowing that because our Savior was forsaken for us, we who are united to him will never be forsaken.

Dear friend, as we prepare for glory, we must not evade grief. Rather, we must endure it as we hope for the day of no more death, no more mourning, and no more pain (see Rev. 21:4). In this hope, we lean toward eternity, when our mouths will be forever filled with laughter, "our tongue with shouts of joy" (Ps. 126:2).

PRAYER

Comforting Father, how we thank you that you are "near to the brokenhearted," that you save "the crushed in spirit" (Ps. 34:18). Because Jesus bore our griefs, we bring our grief to you, looking forward to the day when we will never bear it again. In Jesus's name, amen.

FURTHER ENCOURAGEMENT

Read Isaiah 53; Psalm 126.
Watch "Clarissa Moll: Surprised by Grief" on Open to Hope.

FOR REFLECTION

What have you learned about grief that gives you hope? What have you learned that helps you to offer hope to a grieving friend?

36

What is lament, and how does it help us to face dying and death?

My God, my God, why have you forsaken me? (*Ps.* 22:1)

When Nancy, a servant in a parachurch organization, was diagnosed with a fatal neuroendocrine tumor, she and her husband Glen invited their small group to join them on their journey of grief. As Mark Vroegop tells the story in his book *Dark Clouds, Deep Mercy*, this group learned to lament together. Lament is a special language of prayer that makes up a little over a third of the Psalms, the entire book of Lamentations, and many other parts of the Bible. Vroegop describes the purpose of lament: "Christians affirm that the world is broken, God is powerful, and he will be faithful. Therefore, lament stands in the gap between pain and promise."[1]

> Art thou sore distressed?
> "Come to me," saith One,
> "and coming, be at rest."
> **Stephen of Mar Sabas**

Biblical lament usually follows a pattern of turning to God, naming our grief, asking for help, and renewing confidence in God. Let's follow this pattern through one psalm of lament, Psalm 22.

Turning to God. While we often turn away from God in our grief and pain, David, the author of Psalm 22, turns toward him: "My God, my God, why have you forsaken me? . . . O my God, I cry by day, but you do not answer" (Ps. 22:1–2). David directs his complaint to God, demonstrating his faith in God's care.

Naming our grief. "Why have you forsaken me? . . . You do not answer, and . . . I find no rest" (Ps. 22:1–2). As we name our grief, we note how our current experience doesn't seem to match our understanding of God's goodness and mercy.

Asking for help. After naming his grief, David remembers God's past redemption and boldly asks for help: "In you our fathers trusted . . . and you delivered them. . . . From my mother's womb you have been my God. Be not far from me, for trouble is near, and there is none to help" (Ps. 22:4, 10–11). Remembering that our Redeemer will one day fully restore all things, we can confidently approach the throne of grace.

Renewing confidence in God. In most biblical laments, the writer praises God and trusts in his goodness: "In the midst of the congregation I will praise you. . . . For he has not despised or abhorred the affliction of the afflicted" (Ps. 22:22, 24). This renewed confidence often comes before a change in circumstances and rests in the hope of God's promised deliverance.

As we face sickness and death, we need not suffer silently. The Bible gives voice to our lament. As Clarissa Moll attests, "Since [my husband] Rob died, lament has been my sorrowful tune, yet beneath the melody has run the steady harmony of longing, the sweet refrain of praise."[2] In our lament, we turn our hearts toward the day in eternal glory when our tears will be wiped away in the tender presence of our Lord.

PRAYER

Faithful God, at times, we cry out to you and feel that you do not answer us. Because we know that you have already rescued and redeemed us through our Lord Jesus Christ, we lament, trusting you in our pain. In Jesus's name, amen.

FURTHER ENCOURAGEMENT

Read Psalm 22, 77, 88; Lamentations 1–5.
Watch "How to Lament after Two Years of Loss" with Mark Vroegop.

FOR REFLECTION

Try writing a biblical lament. Include all four aspects of lament (see above). After writing the lament, take a few minutes to describe your experience.

37

What is anticipatory grief?

And being in agony he prayed more earnestly; and his sweat became like great drops of blood falling down to the ground. (*Luke* 22:44)

Three years ago, Lara's father was diagnosed with Alzheimer's. As his only child, Lara is struggling. She finds herself crying frequently, losing her temper daily, and feeling constantly anxious. Like many loved ones of those who have a progressive or terminal disease, Lara is experiencing anticipatory grief. As bereavement counselor Marty Tousley explains, "Extended illness, disability, severe accidental injury, a terminal diagnosis, or the aging and decline of an elderly family member can produce . . . anticipatory grief."[1]

> Hold thou thy cross
> before my closing eyes;
> shine through the gloom,
> and point me to the skies;
> heaven's morning breaks,
> and earth's vain shadows flee;
> in life, in death,
> O Lord, abide with me.
> **Henry Francis Lyte**

Symptoms of anticipatory grief include anger, anxiety, depression, denial, guilt, irritability, and difficulty concentrating. But the grief may be tinged with a sense of hope or comfort: caregivers may imagine relief from their caregiving burden, while the sick may anticipate an end to their suffering. As we consider how to navigate anticipatory grief, we look to Jesus, who experienced it before his crucifixion.

The night before his death, Jesus took refuge in the garden of Gethsemane. The disciples followed him there, but he told them to wait and pray while he went on alone. He knelt, and he cried out. He lamented. He begged God to "remove this cup" (Luke 22:42). In his humanity, Jesus dreaded the horror of crucifixion; he dreaded even more bearing his Father's wrath for our sins. Even so, he prayed, "Not my will, but yours, be done" (v. 42). The Father did not remove the cup, but he did send an angel to strengthen Jesus (see v. 43). And yet, even after the angel came, Jesus cried and prayed more, sweating blood in his agony (see v. 44).

In this poignant scene, we learn much about how to navigate anticipatory grief. Here are four things we can do.

Name the horror of death. "Jesus was averse to death," theologian Philip Ryken notes.[2] Death, as we observed in the first reflection, came as a result of the fall, and it is normal for us to grieve as it approaches.

Pray and invite others to pray. Jesus prayed an honest lament, naming his sorrow and fear. He also asked the disciples to pray, even though he knew they would fail. We too can lament and cry out to God. And because grief may numb us and mute our prayers, we can ask others to pray for us.

Invite others to bear your burdens. Just as Jesus invited his disciples to pray for him as he cried out to God, we can reach out and receive help from others, including Jesus, our burden-bearer.

Even as you feel anticipatory grief, anticipate glory. Hebrews 12:2 tells us that Jesus endured the cross "for the joy that was set before him," the joy of being united with us eternally. We too have joy awaiting us: our eternal future with Christ in glory.

Friend, in hard days of decline, may you remember that you need not bear your grief alone, and that you will not bear it forever. Lean into glory, even as you grieve.

PRAYER

Suffering Savior, what wondrous love you have shown in sharing your grief with us. As we anticipate decline and death, help us to find rest in your warm embrace. In your compassionate name, amen.

FURTHER ENCOURAGEMENT

Read Luke 22:29–46.
Read "Coping as You Anticipate a Loss" by Marty Tousley.

FOR REFLECTION

Have you or someone you know experienced anticipatory grief? Which of the suggested approaches might help you or your friend?

38

How do we grieve when we don't know a loved one's eternal destiny?

Shall not the Judge of all the earth do what is just? (*Gen.* 18:25)

When my dad was diagnosed with terminal cancer, I feared that he was not a believer. For years I had prayed for his salvation, and whenever I could do so without offending him, I asked about his beliefs. On more than one occasion, he told me that he believed "all roads lead up to the top of the mountain." That sounded to me like a clear denial of Jesus's claim "I am the way, and the truth, and the life. No one comes to the Father except through me" (John 14:6).

When forever from our sight
pass the stars, the day, the night,
Lord of angels, on our eyes
let eternal morning rise,
and shadows end.
Mary A. Lathbury

Over the two years that my father lived with cancer, I began to see his heart soften. One day, while waiting to see his oncologist, he told me about living in San Diego, where his dad was stationed in the navy. He mentioned that he had been baptized there as a ten-year-old. Shortly after that conversation, I gave him a Bible, realizing that he didn't have one, and he gently teased me about joining me at the ladies' Bible study. In following days, whenever I saw him, he half-jokingly asked me to help him to understand Thessalonians.

My dad entered the latter stages of dying even as we were awaiting the results of the biopsy of our son's brain tumor. On the day we learned that our son's tumor was not cancerous, I texted my dad, and he responded, "To God be the glory." Two weeks later, he died.

For years, I had dreaded his death because I had no assurance about whether I would see him in heaven. But God gave me peace. Still no certainty—there was no way I could know for sure. But I had peace.

Author and theologian Nancy Guthrie points out three truths to consider when we're uncertain about a dying love one's salvation.

We can never perfectly evaluate another person's heart. We are looking for the fruit that characterizes the life of a believer, but we may see little to none. For example, the repentant thief on the cross trusted in Christ just before he died—he never had an opportunity to cultivate other fruit (see Luke 23:39–43).

God is trustworthy. Genesis 18:25 says, "Shall not the Judge of all the earth do what is just?" The answer is yes. We can trust him to judge fairly.

God is rich in mercy. As Guthrie says, "He loves to save. We often have hurdles we want people to jump through to believe that they have been joined to Christ. We are often stingy with mercy."[1] God is far more merciful than we are.

Dear friend, if you are unsure about a dying loved one's faith, I encourage you to grieve with hope in the God who is just and merciful. Yes, we must wait to see what will be revealed in eternal glory. But we can trust that God is kind and gracious, and that he will wipe away every tear in the new heavens and the new earth.

PRAYER

Holy and just Father, may you have mercy on our loved ones. Bring them to bow before Jesus as their loving Savior. Give us wisdom and peace as we walk alongside them. In Jesus's redeeming name, amen.

FURTHER ENCOURAGEMENT

Read Exodus 34:6; Luke 23:39–43; Ephesians 2:4.
Listen to "Comfort When an Unbeliever Dies" with Nancy Guthrie.

FOR REFLECTION

Are you concerned about a loved one's salvation? Write a prayer, asking God to bring you comfort and peace in your grief. Ask him for wisdom and words to speak to a dying loved one about the hope of the gospel.

39

How do we help someone who is grieving?

The Lord *is near to the brokenhearted and saves the crushed in spirit.* (*Ps.* 34:18)

Miriam Neff, founder and president of a ministry to widows, notes that "widows lose 75 percent of their friendship network when they lose a spouse."[1] Couple friends often fall away once the husband is gone, some friends shy away from the widow's grief, and other friends maintained their relationship through an interest the widow no longer has now that her spouse is gone. Clarissa Moll said that she and her family struggled to attend worship on Sunday mornings, even though her church had cared well for her family's emotional, spiritual, and material needs. Moll surveyed other grieving people and found that she was not alone. Many struggle to fit in at church when they have lost a loved one.[2] As the body of Christ, we must find ways to comfort and support the grieving.

We take our cue from Jesus, who did this perfectly. As we saw in question 31, Jesus listened carefully to both Martha's and Mary's expressions of grief over the death of their brother Lazarus, and he responded to their unique needs individually (see John 11:20–37). Jesus was so deeply troubled by Lazarus's death and his friends' grief that he wept, even though he knew he would soon raise Lazarus and reverse the curse of death (see vv. 33–35). In Christ's strength, and through the work of the Holy Spirit, we can comfort others as we have been comforted, even if we have not experienced the same kind of loss.

> Death cannot destroy forever;
> from our fears, cares, and tears
> it will us deliver.
> It will close life's mournful story,
> make a way that we
> may enter heav'nly glory.
> **Paul Gerhardt**

As we come alongside the grieving, there are a few things we want to avoid. We do not minimize a person's loss by saying things like, "Oh, well, at least she was ninety-three" or "Just think how happy he is in heaven!" We do not compare our stories of loss and suffering with those of the grieving person. We do not rush people through their grief. We do not avoid or ignore the grieving person, even if we are afraid of saying the wrong thing.

Instead, we listen to the grieving person and validate their suffering. We invite the grieving person to lament, and we can join in their lament (see question 36). We offer our physical presence while remaining sensitive to the grieving person's need for alone time. We recognize that the grieving person will eventually make the difficult choice to release some of their grief, and that "to think less, feel less, and invest less in [their] grief feels like a betrayal to the person who died."[3] As we recognize that struggle, we give the grieving person permission to let go, but we do not rush them toward that day. At the right time and in the right context, we should point the grieving person to biblical hope. We can then ask the grieving person if it would be okay if we prayed with them or sent them a written or voice-recorded prayer. Even though we may not know what to do or say, we can always find wisdom by asking the Holy Spirit to guide us as we comfort the grieving.

Dear friend, look around your church on a Sunday morning. Who is actively grieving? Who has lost a loved one in recent months or years? Because you have the hope of heaven, you can confidently and compassionately engage their grief, offering them the comfort of Christ.

PRAYER

Loving Jesus, make our churches hospitals for the wounded. Forgive us for the ways we have failed to care for the grieving. Help us to seek out the grieving and to serve them courageously, kindly, and compassionately. In your name, amen.

FURTHER ENCOURAGEMENT

Read Psalms 34:18; 56:8; John 11; 2 Corinthians 1:3–7.
Listen to "What Grieving People Wish You Knew" with Nancy Guthrie.

FOR REFLECTION

Think of a person you know who is grieving. Choose one or two ways to walk with them in their grief. Write down a date by which you plan to complete this action.

Part Seven

Ending Well

40

How do we prepare for glory in the midst of grief?

So we do not lose heart. Though our outer self is wasting away, our inner self is being renewed day by day. For this light momentary affliction is preparing for us an eternal weight of glory beyond all comparison, as we look not to the things that are seen but to the things that are unseen. (2 Cor. 4:16–18)

We have faced death, and we have found it lacking. As John Donne famously put it in "Holy Sonnet X":

> One short sleep past, we wake eternally
> And death shall be no more; Death, thou shalt die.[1]

Yes, as our outer selves waste away, we will know grief. And yet, as the apostle Paul promises, a day is coming (and in Revelation 22:7 our Lord says it is coming soon) when grief will give way to glory—eternal, shining glory.

In that day of "no more . . . mourning, nor crying, nor pain" (Rev. 21:4), this book will be obsolete. You will never again get a call telling you that your father is in the emergency room after a fall. You will never again be faced with fraught decisions about end-of-life care. You will never again face the grief of dementia or heart disease, cancer or chemo. You will never again have nightmares about your child's death. All suffering and sorrow will have come to an end.

Grief will give way to glory. Jesus will return to raise our bodies to eternal life in our eternal home: the new heavens and the new earth. In this place, the "leaves of the tree [of life will be] for the healing of nations" (Rev. 22:2). In this place, we will see our Savior's face. As our hearts no longer clouded by sin take in the full breadth and depth of his glory, we will finally and fully be like him (see 1 John 3:2). In his presence, we will spend eternity fulfilling our greatest purpose: enjoying "the immeasurable riches of [God's] grace in kindness toward us in Christ Jesus" (Eph. 2:7). Theologian Dane Ortlund writes, "One day God is going to walk us through the wardrobe into Narnia, and we will stand there, paralyzed with joy, wonder, astonishment, and relief. . . . As we stand there, we will never be scolded for the sins of this life, never looked at askance, and never told, 'Enjoy this, but remember you don't deserve this.' The very point of heaven and eternity is to enjoy his 'grace in kindness.'"[2]

I need thee, precious Jesus,
and hope to see thee soon,
encircled with the rainbow
and seated on thy throne.
There, with thy blood-bought children,
my joy shall ever be,
to sing my Jesus' praises,
to gaze, O Lord, on thee.
Fredrick Whitfield

Dear friend, we are surely going to die. But, oh, what glories and grace await us when we do! We need not fear. Our hero, our Savior King, our beloved Bridegroom, stands ready to take our hand, to bring us to the Father, to announce with joy, "Here is my beloved, your precious child." Because of this great hope, we can indeed confidently, calmly, courageously, and compassionately prepare for glory.

PRAYER

Heavenly Father, thank you for showing us the glory that awaits. We cry out with all the saints, "Come quickly, Lord Jesus!" How we long for the day when we will enjoy your immeasurable riches and begin serving you in glory forever and ever. In Jesus's glorious name, amen.

FURTHER ENCOURAGEMENT

Read 2 Corinthians 4:7–18; Revelation 22.
Watch "Randy Alcorn's Message at His Wife Nanci's Memorial Service" on Eternal Perspective Ministries.

FOR REFLECTION

What do you hope for as you approach the end of this journey? How will you continue to prepare for glory?

Acknowledgments

Writing this book has challenged me on every level. God has given me a whole cloud of faithful witnesses to cheer me on as I cross the finish line. I am grateful for . . .

My Lord and Savior Jesus Christ.

My husband, Kirby Loftin Turnage III, my beloved for over forty years. How I love living this legacy of our truest hope with you.

Our children and grandchildren. How beautifully you live the story of our hope of glory: Robert Reynolds Turnage; Mary Elizabeth, Caleb, Everett, and Augusta Blake; Jackie, Matt, and Reed Roelofs; and Kirby, Amy Anne, and Birdie Turnage.

My in-laws, Kirby and Joy Turnage, for your loving support.

Dear friends who consistently point me toward the hope of glory: Mary Baker, Jennie Carter, Anne Henegar, Cindy Jank, Kelly Markham, Hope Parker, Cheryl Simcox, Scotty and Darlene Smith, and Christie Tilley.

The many people who prayed for this work, read early chapters, and offered insight and encouragement along the way, especially Sheryll Jo Biles, Susan Calderazzo, Lauri Hogle, Cindy Jank, Patsy Kuipers, Kelly Markham, Suzy Marshall, Peggy Orren, Hope Parker, and Jan Thomae.

Women's ministry leaders: Karen Hodge and Kathy Wargo, for assuring me that this work was needed.

The professors at Covenant Theological Seminary who guided me as I created this project for the Doctor of Ministry program: Dr. Joel Hathaway, my advisor, who suggested the title *Preparing for Glory*, and Dr. Jeremy Ruckstaetter, who supervised my independent study on death, dying, and the afterlife.

The body of our local church, Pinewoods Presbyterian, faithfully led by our wonderful pastor, Joel Treick, and his delightful wife, Kate.

The team at P&R Publishing: David Almack, Amanda Martin, and all the others who came alongside me to make this offering strong and beautiful.

And last, but not least, you, my readers. Many of you have connected with me over the years to share your stories. Some of you are new to me, and I look forward to knowing you better. Feel free to stay in touch at etlivingstory@gmail.com. If you'd like to receive my monthly newsletter with free resources on aging, caregiving, legacy, and end-of-life issues, please sign up here: http://eepurl.com/b__teX. My prayers are with you as you prepare for your glorious end—which is, after all, the true beginning.

Notes

Introduction: Preparing for Glory

1. See the Heidelberg Catechism, question and answer 1.

Chapter One: What is glory, and do we really need to prepare for it?

1. Charles Haddon Spurgeon, "Glory!" (speech, May 20, 1883), The Spurgeon Center, https://www.spurgeon.org/resource-library/sermons/glory/#flipbook/.

Chapter Four: What hope does the resurrection of Christ give us?

1. "Resurrection Did Not Happen, Say Quarter of Christians," *BBC* News, April 9, 2017, https://www.bbc.com/news/uk-england-39153121.
2. Gary R. Habermas and Antony Flew, *Did the Resurrection Happen? A Conversation with Gary Habermas and Antony Flew* (Downers Grove, IL: InterVarsity Press, 2009), 85. Quoted in Stephen T. Um, *1 Corinthians: The Word of the Cross*, Preaching the Word (Wheaton, IL: Crossway, 2015), 373.

Chapter Five: What happens to us when we die?

1. Philip Graham Ryken, *Luke*, Reformed Expository Commentary (Phillipsburg, NJ: P&R Publishing, 2009), 2:199.
2. Study note for 2 Corinthians 12:3, *ESV Study Bible* (Wheaton, IL: Crossway, 2008), 2238.

Chapter Six: Do we become angels when we die?

1. J. I. Packer, *Concise Theology: A Guide to Historic Christian Beliefs* (Carol Stream, IL: Tyndale House, 1993), 67. Packer cites 2 Peter 2:4 and Jude 6.

Chapter Nine: What does Christ's resurrection mean for the future of our bodies?

1. Kate Golembiewski, "Life after Death? Cryonicists Try to Defy Mortality by Freezing Bodies," *Discover Magazine*, October 14, 2022, https://www.discovermagazine.com/technology/will-cryonically-frozen-bodies-ever-be-brought-back-to-life.
2. Golembiewski, "Life after Death?"
3. Dennis Kowalski, quoted in Golembiewski, "Life after Death?"
4. Paul R. Williamson, *Death and the Afterlife: Biblical Perspectives on Ultimate Questions*, New Studies in Biblical Theology (Downers Grove, IL: IVP Academic, 2018), 135.

Chapter Ten: What are the new heavens and the new earth?

1. N. T. Wright, *Surprised by Hope: Rethinking Heaven, the Resurrection, and the Mission of the Church* (New York: HarperOne, 2008), 151.
2. Gerhard Kittel, Gerhard Friedrich, and Geoffrey W. Bromiley, eds., *Theological Dictionary of the New Testament: Abridged in One Volume* (Grand Rapids: Eerdmans, 1985), 388.
3. Nathan L. K. Bierma, *Bringing Heaven down to Earth: Connecting This Life to the Next* (Phillipsburg, NJ: P&R Publishing, 2005), 44.

Chapter Eleven: What will life be like in the new heavens and the new earth?

1. Simon Trump and Adam Lusher, "The Queen Grants Heart Girl's Wish on Anniversary Day," *Telegraph*, June 1, 2003, https://www.telegraph.co.uk/news/uknews/1431632/The-Queen-grants-heart-girls-wish-on-anniversary-day.html.

Chapter Twelve: What happens to the believer on the day of judgment?

1. Richard D. Phillips, *Revelation*, Reformed Expository Commentary (Phillipsburg, NJ: P&R Publishing, 2017), 604.
2. Darrell W. Johnson, *Discipleship on the Edge: An Expository Journey through the Book of Revelation* (Vancouver: Regent College Publishing, 2004), 356.
3. Nancy Guthrie, *Blessed: Experiencing the Promise of the Book of Revelation* (Wheaton, IL: Crossway, 2022), 218.

Chapter Thirteen: What happens to the unbeliever on the day of judgment?

1. Thankfully, I saw my mother turn to Christ in her later years, and I have reason to hope that my father did the same before he died.
2. J. I. Packer, *Knowing God*, 20th anniversary ed. (Downers Grove, IL: InterVarsity Press, 1993), 151.
3. Jonathan Edwards, quoted in Dane C. Ortlund, *Gentle and Lowly: The Heart of Christ for Sinners and Sufferers* (Wheaton, IL: Crossway, 2020), 142.
4. Packer, *Knowing God*, 153.
5. For more on this concept, see Scotty Smith, *Revelation: Hope in the Darkness, Study Guide with Leader's Notes*, The Gospel-Centered Life in the Bible (Greensboro, NC: New Growth Press, 2020), 110–111.

Chapter Fourteen: Is hell real, and if so, what is it like?

1. Leslie Schmucker, "The Uncomfortable Subject Jesus Addressed More than Anyone Else," The Gospel Coalition, May 11, 2017, https://www.thegospelcoalition.org/article/the-uncomfortable-subject-jesus-addressed-more-than-anyone-else/.
2. Timothy Keller, "The Importance of Hell," *Timothy Keller* (blog), August 1, 2008, https://timothykeller.com/blog/2008/8/1/the-importance-of-hell.

Chapter Fifteen: Is there an "art" to dying?

1. L. S. Dugdale, *The Lost Art of Dying: Reviving Forgotten Wisdom* (New York: HarperOne, 2020), 21.
2. Dugdale, 21.
3. J. Todd Billings, *The End of the Christian Life: How Embracing Our Mortality Frees Us to Truly Live* (Grand Rapids: Brazos Press, 2020), 141.
4. Allen Verhey, *The Christian Art of Dying: Learning from Jesus* (Grand Rapids: Eerdmans, 2011), loc. 2443.

Chapter Sixteen: What does the Bible teach about the losses of aging?

1. Olga Khazan, "Should We Die?," *The Atlantic*, February 18, 2017, https://www.theatlantic.com/health/archive/2017/02/should-we-die/516357/.
2. Andrew Steele, *Ageless: The New Science of Getting Older without Getting Old* (New York: Doubleday, 2021), 3.
3. Will Willimon, *Aging: Growing Old in Church*, Pastoring for Life: Theological Wisdom for Ministering Well (Grand Rapids: Baker, 2020), 21.

Chapter Seventeen: What does it look like to live wisely and graciously as we age?

1. J. I. Packer, *Finishing Our Course with Joy: Guidance from God for Engaging with Our Aging* (Wheaton, IL: Crossway, 2014), 22.
2. Sam Allberry, *What God Has to Say about Our Bodies: How the Gospel Is Good News for Our Physical Selves* (Wheaton, IL: Crossway, 2021), 185.

Chapter Eighteen: What do sickness and death say about the strength of our faith?

1. Kate Bowler, "Death, the Prosperity Gospel and Me," *The New York Times*, February 13, 2016, https://www.nytimes.com/2016/02/14/opinion/sunday/death-the-prosperity-gospel-and-me.html.
2. Bowler, "Death, the Prosperity Gospel and Me."

3. Crossway Bibles, ed., *Gospel Transformation Study Bible: Christ in All of Scripture, Grace for All of Life* (Wheaton, IL: Crossway, 2013), 1424.

Chapter Nineteen: How do we know which medical means to employ at the end of life?

1. Kathryn Butler, *Between Life and Death: A Gospel-Centered Guide to End-of-Life Medical Care* (Wheaton, IL: Crossway, 2019), 50.
2. Allen Verhey, *The Christian Art of Dying: Learning from Jesus* (Grand Rapids: Eerdmans, 2011), loc. 1.
3. L. S. Dugdale, *The Lost Art of Dying: Reviving Forgotten Wisdom* (New York: HarperOne, 2020), 6.
4. Dugdale, 11.
5. Bill Davis, *Departing in Peace: Biblical Decision-Making at the End of Life* (Phillipsburg, NJ: P&R Publishing, 2017), 37.

Chapter Twenty: What information and documents do we need to gather to prepare our loved ones for our incapacitation or death?

1. Bill Davis, *Departing in Peace: Biblical Decision-Making at the End of Life* (Phillipsburg, NJ: P&R Publishing, 2017), 32.

Chapter Twenty-One: What arrangements should we make for our bodies after our death?

1. Russell Moore, quoted in Joe Carter, "The FAQs: What Christians Should Know about Cremation," The Gospel Coalition, September 20, 2017, https://www.thegospelcoalition.org/article/the-faqs-what-christians-should-know-about-cremation/.

Chapter Twenty-Two: What kind of end-of-life service should we have?

1. John Leland, "It's My Funeral and I'll Serve Ice Cream If I Want To," *The New York Times*, July 20, 2006, https://www.nytimes.com/2006/07/20/fashion/20funeral.html.
2. Rob Moll, *The Art of Dying: Living Fully into the Life to Come* (Downers Grove, IL: InterVarsity Press, 2021), 203–4.

3. See Eugene H. Peterson, *Conversations: The Message with Its Translator* (Colorado Springs: NavPress, 2007), 1810.

Chapter Twenty-Three: What does the Bible say about stewarding our financial legacy?

1. See Tremper Longman III, *Proverbs*, Baker Commentary on the Old Testament Wisdom and Psalms (Grand Rapids: Baker Publishing Group, 2006), 573–76.
2. See Eugene H. Peterson, *Conversations: The Message with Its Translator* (Colorado Springs: NavPress, 2007), 1810.
3. Adam Zylstra, "Giving When You're Gone," The Gospel Coalition, November 16, 2022, https://www.thegospelcoalition.org/article/giving-gone/.
4. Zylstra, "Giving When You're Gone."

Chapter Twenty-Four: How do we let go of all the "stuff" we have accumulated?

1. Adele Ahlberg Calhoun, *Spiritual Disciplines Handbook: Practices That Transform Us* (Downers Grove, IL: InterVarsity Press, 2015), 85.

Chapter Twenty-Six: What is an emotional legacy, and how do we leave one?

1. Ira Byock, *The Four Things That Matter Most—10th Anniversary Edition: A Book about Living* (New York: Free Press, 2004), 7.

Chapter Twenty-Eight: Why is it important to express our gratitude as we or a loved one nears the end of life?

1. Polly Drew, "Interview with Katy Butler, prominent author, journalist," *Milwaukee Journal Sentinel*, August 1, 2014, https://archive.jsonline.com/entertainment/books/interview-with-katy-butler-prominent-author-journalist-b99319290z1-269581141.html/.
2. Amy Ryland, "The Thank You Project," *Lunch Lady*, November 27, 2021, https://hellolunchlady.com.au/blogs/blog/the-thank-you-project.

Chapter Twenty-Nine: How does being part of a church help us to care for the sick and dying?

1. L. S. Dugdale, *The Lost Art of Dying: Reviving Forgotten Wisdom* (New York: HarperOne, 2020), 68.

Chapter Thirty-One: How can we care for caregivers?

1. Richard Schulz and Paula R. Sherwood, "Physical and Mental Health Effects of Family Caregiving," *American Journal of Nursing* 108, no. 9 (September 2008): 23–27, https://www.ncbi.nlm.nih.gov/pmc/articles/PMC2791523/.
2. Marissa Bondurant, *Who Cares for You?: A 4 Week Bible Study for Caregivers* (San Antonio: Marissa Bondurant, 2022), 10.

Chapter Thirty-Two: How do I care for myself as a caregiver?

1. Richard Schulz and Scott R. Beach, "Caregiving as a Risk Factor for Mortality: The Caregiver Health Effects Study," *JAMA* 282, no. 23 (December 15, 1999): 2215–19, https://doi.org/10.1001/jama.282.23.2215.

Chapter Thirty-Four: How does prayer prepare us for glory?

1. Eric Tonjes, *Either Way, We'll Be All Right: An Honest Exploration of God in Our Grief* (Colorado Springs: NavPress, 2021), 52.
2. Michael Hoppe, interview by author, September 12, 2022.

Chapter Thirty-Five: How can we cope with the physical, spiritual, and emotional impacts of grief?

1. Clarissa Moll, *Beyond the Darkness: A Gentle Guide for Living with Grief and Thriving after Loss* (Carol Stream, IL: Tyndale House, 2022), 116–17.

Chapter Thirty-Six: What is lament, and how does it help us face dying and death?

1. Mark Vroegop, *Dark Clouds, Deep Mercy: Discovering the Grace of Lament* (Wheaton, IL: Crossway, 2019), 28.
2. Clarissa Moll, *Beyond the Darkness: A Gentle Guide for Living with Grief and Thriving after Loss* (Carol Stream, IL: Tyndale House, 2022), 195.

Chapter Thirty-Seven: What is anticipatory grief?

1. Marty Tousley, "Coping as You Anticipate a Loss," Open to Hope, June 2, 2009, https://www.opentohope.com/coping-as-you-anticipate-a-loss/.
2. Philip Graham Ryken, *Luke*, Reformed Expository Commentary (Phillipsburg, NJ: P&R Publishing, 2009), 2:501.

Chapter Thirty-Eight: How do we grieve when we don't know a loved one's eternal destiny?

1. Nancy Guthrie, "Comfort When an Unbeliever Dies," The Gospel Coalition, May 30, 2017, https://www.thegospelcoalition.org/podcasts/tgc-podcast/comfort-when-an-unbeliever-dies/.

Chapter Thirty-Nine: How do we help someone who is grieving?

1. Miriam Neff, "The Widow's Might," *Christianity Today*, January 18, 2008, https://www.christianitytoday.com/ct/2008/january/26.42.html.
2. Clarissa Moll, *Beyond the Darkness: A Gentle Guide for Living with Grief and Thriving after Loss* (Carol Stream, IL: Tyndale House, 2022), 181.
3. Nancy Guthrie, *What Grieving People Wish You Knew about What Really Helps (and What Really Hurts)* (Wheaton, IL: Crossway, 2016), 180.

Chapter Forty: How do we prepare for glory in the midst of grief?

1. John Donne, "Holy Sonnets: Death, be not proud," Poetry Foundation, https://www.poetryfoundation.org/poems/44107/holy-sonnets-death-be-not-proud.
2. Dane C. Ortlund, *Gentle and Lowly: The Heart of Christ for Sinners and Sufferers* (Wheaton, IL: Crossway, 2020), 209.

Recommended Resources

In addition to the resources mentioned in each reflection, the following books and websites may be helpful in exploring these topics further.

Alcorn, Randy C. *Heaven*. Wheaton, IL: Tyndale House, 2004. [Alcorn's book delves deeply into many of the questions people have about heaven, as well as the new heavens and the new earth.] (**heaven, new heavens and new earth**)

Betters, Sharon W., and Susan Hunt. *Aging with Grace: Flourishing in an Anti-Aging Culture*. Wheaton, IL: Crossway, 2021. [Betters and Hunt beautifully demonstrate what it looks like to age with grace, interviewing various women who have done so.] (**aging, gospel-centered**)

Bondurant, Marissa. *Who Cares for You? A 4 Week Bible Study for Caregivers*. San Antonio: Marissa Bondurant, 2022. [Bondurant offers a kind gift to caregivers, a wonderful study that could be used in a caregivers' support group.] (**caregiving**)

Butler, Kathryn. *Between Life and Death: A Gospel-Centered Guide to End-of-Life Medical Care*. Wheaton, IL: Crossway, 2019. [Butler, a former critical care surgeon, offers biblical wisdom and medical knowledge to guide end-of-life medical decisions.] (**end-of-life medical decisions**)

Byock, Ira. *The Four Things That Matter Most—10th Anniversary Edition: A Book about Living*. New York: Simon and Schuster, 2004. [Byock, a leader in palliative care, shares practical wisdom about emotional legacies.] (**emotional legacy**)

Carter, Joe. "The FAQs: What Christians Should Know about Cremation." The Gospel Coalition. September 20, 2017. https://www.thegospelcoalition.org/article/the-faqs-what-christians-should-know-about-cremation/. [Carter explains the pros and cons of burial and cremation.] (**practical legacy, disposition of body**)

Davis, Bill. *Departing in Peace: Biblical Decision-Making at the End of Life*. Phillipsburg, NJ: P&R Publishing, 2017. [Davis walks us through a biblical decision-making process for various situations we may encounter at the end of life. He also offers wisdom about many issues surrounding practical legacy.] (**practical legacy, advance directives, end-of-life medical care, memorial services, disposition of body**)

Dugdale, L. S. *The Lost Art of Dying: Reviving Forgotten Wisdom*. New York: HarperCollins, 2020. [Dugdale, a physician, urges us to prepare for death, focusing on the virtues needed to do so.] (**preparing for death, practical legacy, end-of-life medical care**)

Dunlop, John. *Finishing Well to the Glory of God: Strategies from a Christian Physician*. Wheaton, IL: Crossway, 2011. [Dunlop, a Christian physician specializing in geriatrics, offers biblical hope and sound wisdom for aging well.] (**aging, end-of-life medical care**)

Fields, Leslie Leyland. *Your Story Matters: Finding, Writing, and Living the Truth of Your Life*. Colorado Springs: NavPress, 2020. [Fields helps us understand that our stories matter to God and encourages us to record them.] (**spiritual legacy**)

Guthrie, Nancy. "Please Don't Make My Funeral All About Me." The Gospel Coalition. April 8, 2014. https://www.thegospelcoalition.org/article/please-dont-make-my-funeral-all-about-me/. [Guthrie describes the Christian hope for funerals and other end-of-life services.] (**funerals**)

———. *What Grieving People Wish You Knew about What Really Helps (and What Really Hurts)*. Wheaton, IL: Crossway, 2016. [Guthrie, who lost two infant children, offers specific guidance for how to love the grieving. A brief book and a powerful guide.] (**grief, caring for the grieving**)

Keller, Timothy. "The Importance of Hell." *Timothy Keller* (blog). August 1, 2008. https://timothykeller.com/blog/2008/8/1/the-importance-of-hell. [Keller clearly and concisely explains biblical teaching about hell.] (**hell, judgment**)

Moll, Clarissa. *Beyond the Darkness: A Gentle Guide for Living with Grief and Thriving after Loss*. Carol Stream, IL: Tyndale House, 2022. [Moll, a young widow, guides us through the journey of grief, offering spiritual and practical wisdom—including a chapter on understanding children's grief—and urging us not to rush the process.] (**grief**)

Packer, J. I. *Finishing Our Course with Joy: Guidance from God for Engaging with Our Aging*. Wheaton, IL: Crossway, 2014. [Packer, a renowned theologian who wrote this book at age eighty-eight, urges us to "Live for God one day at a time," stressing that the "final sprint, so I urge, should be a sprint indeed."] (**aging, dying**)

———. *Knowing God*. Downers Grove, IL: InterVarsity Press, 1993. [Packer's great work offers concise and biblical coverage of many of the theological topics in this book.] (**mortality, resurrection, angels**)

Schmucker, Leslie. "The Uncomfortable Subject Jesus Addressed More than Anyone Else." The Gospel Coalition. May 11, 2017. https://www.thegospelcoalition.org/article/the-uncomfortable-subject-jesus-addressed-more-than-anyone-else/. [Schmucker brilliantly explains how understanding hell helps us better appreciate the gospel.] (**hell**)

Smith, Scotty. *Revelation: Hope in the Darkness, Study Guide with Leader's Notes*. Greensboro, NC: New Growth Press, 2020. [Smith gives us a simple, readable guide to one of the more difficult books of the Bible, helping us to see that Revelation is all about Jesus and the hope that awaits us when he returns.] (**new heavens and new earth, resurrection, judgment**)

Spurgeon, Charles. "Glory!" The Spurgeon Center. May 20, 1883. https://www.spurgeon.org/resource-library/sermons/glory/. [Spurgeon's beautiful sermon whets our appetite for eternal glory.] (**glory**)

StoryCorps.org [StoryCorps helps people to tell their stories and interview others about their own. At its website, you will find numerous questions to help you recall stories from your life.] (**spiritual legacy**)

Taylor, Daniel. *Creating a Spiritual Legacy: How to Share Your Stories, Values, and Wisdom*. Grand Rapids: Brazos Press, 2011. [Taylor guides and motivates us to record our spiritual legacies in a variety of ways.] (**spiritual legacy**)

Turnage, Elizabeth. *Numbering Your Days.* https://elizabethturnagenumberingdays.substack.com/ [In this free monthly column, I offer gospel-centered, biblical wisdom for issues of caregiving, aging, and dying.] (**aging, caregiving, legacy, end-of-life**)

———. *The Waiting Room: 60 Meditations for Finding Peace & Hope in a Health Crisis.* Living Story: 2019. [In this devotional, I offer biblical hope for caregivers and patients in a health crisis.] (**caregiving, grief**)

Vroegop, Mark. *Dark Clouds, Deep Mercy: Discovering the Grace of Lament.* Wheaton, IL: Crossway, 2019. [Vroegop teaches us how to follow the biblical pattern of lament as we grieve.] (**lament, grief**)

Zylstra, Adam. "Giving When You're Gone." The Gospel Coalition. November 16, 2022. https://www.thegospelcoalition.org/article/giving-gone/. [Zylstra offers practical and biblical wisdom for financial stewardship.] (**financial legacy**)

A *Preparing for Glory* Playlist

"All Things New," Steven Curtis Chapman
"Come Lift Up Your Sorrows," Michael Card
"Day of the Lord (Psalm 37)," Wendell Kimbrough
"Death, Be Not Proud," Audrey Assad
"Dust We Are and Shall Return," The Brilliance
"The Glory Hymn," Simple Hymns
"He Will," Ellie Holcomb
"His Eye Is on the Sparrow," Keith & Kristyn Getty, Heather Headley
"Home," Chris Tomlin
"How Sweet and Aweful Is the Place," Sovereign Grace Music, Bob Kauflin
"Jesus, What a Friend for Sinners," Matthew Smith
"The Old Rugged Cross," Alan Jackson
"Pass Me Not, O Gentle Savior," Red Mountain Church
"Resurrection Day," Rend Collective
"Scars in Heaven," Casting Crowns
"See, What a Morning," Keith & Kristyn Getty
"Soon and Very Soon," Andrae Crouch
"Stay with Me – Bleibet Hier," Taizé
"Tis So Sweet," Shane & Shane
"Treasure of Jesus," Steven Curtis Chapman
"Warrior," Sojourn

Index of Scripture Readings

Numbers in parentheses signify chapters.

Elizabeth Reynolds Turnage is a gospel life and legacy coach, author, and speaker. She helps people live, prepare, and share their legacy to bring hope to future generations. She cofounded the Numbering Your Days Network to share gospel encouragement for aging, caregiving, legacy, grief, and end of life. Elizabeth and her husband, Kip, enjoy feasting and sharing good stories with their four adult children, their children-in-law, and their young grandchildren.